EXPLANATION.

The Capitals of States thus .... *
Principal Cities and Towns .... ●
Turnpike Roads _____
Principal travelling roads _____
Common roads _____
Canals _____ Rail Roads...........
The figures along the Roads indicate
the Distances in miles from Place to
Place.

MITCHELL'S
TRAVELLERS GUIDE
THROUGH THE
UNITED STATES.
A Map
OF THE
ROADS, DISTANCES, STEAM BOAT
& CANAL ROUTES &c.
BY J. H. YOUNG
Philadelphia.
Published by
S. AUGUSTUS MITCHELL.
1832

ENGRAVED ON STEEL BY J. H. YOUNG & D. HAINES.

WHERE WE LIVED

WHERE WE LIVED

Discovering the Places We Once Called Home

THE AMERICAN HOME FROM 1775 TO 1840

JACK LARKIN

The Taunton Press

(fronitispiece) A drawing room containing two Windsor chairs in the 1739 Great Barrington, Massachusetts, house of Gen. Joseph Dwight. Also in this house, the great romantic poet William Cullen Bryant was married to Lucy Fairchild.

The Taunton Press
Inspiration for hands-on living®

The Taunton Press, Inc.,
63 South Main Street, PO Box 5506,
Newtown, Connecticut 06470-5506
e-mail: tp@taunton.com

Editor: Steve Culpepper
Jacket/Cover design: Chris Thompson
Interior design and layout: Chika Azuma
Inside cover endpapers: *Mitchell's Travellers Guide through the United States,*
courtesy David Rumsey Map Collection, www.davidrumsey.com

LIBRARY OF CONGRESS CATALOGING-IN-PUBLICATION DATA
Larkin, Jack, 1943-
  Where we lived : discovering the places we once called home : the American home from 1775 to 1840 / Jack Larkin.
     p. cm.
  Includes bibliographical references and index.
  ISBN-13: 978-1-56158-847-3 (alk. paper)
  ISBN-10: 1-56158-847-4 (alk. paper)
 1. Historic buildings--United States. 2. Dwellings--United States. 3. Historic buildings--United States--Pictorial works. 4. Dwellings--United States--Pictorial works. 5. United States--History, Local. 6. United States--Description and travel. 7. Travelers' writings. 8. United States--Social life and customs--1783-1865. 9. Home--United States--History. 10. Architecture, Domestic--United States--History. I. Title.

E159.L33 2006
973.5--dc22
                                        2006018124
Printed in the United States of America
10 9 8 7 6 5 4 3 2 1

The National Trust for Historic Preservation is a private, nonprofit membership organization dedicated to saving historic places and revitalizing America's communities. Recipient of the National Humanities Medal, the Trust was founded in 1949 and provides leadership, education, advocacy, and resources to protect the irreplaceable places that tell America's story. Staff at the Washington, D.C. headquarters, six regional offices and 28 historic sites work with the Trust's 270,000 members and thousands of preservation groups in all 50 states. For more information, visit www.nationaltrust.org.

This book is published under the joint imprint of the National Trust for Historic Preservation and The Taunton Press, Inc.

To Barbara
And to the men and women of the Historic American
Buildings Survey, past and present

ACKNOWLEDGMENTS

Many thanks to the Library of Congress. Its American Memory website,
which provides access to all the HABS photographs, drawings, and documents, is
a superlative example of public money well spent. And unless otherwise noted,
all the photographs in this book are from the Library of Congress, Prints &
Photographs Division, Historic American Buildings Survey.

Thanks also go to Old Sturbridge Village, which has generously allowed use of
photographs from its collections.

The author also thanks Steve Culpepper of The Taunton Press, who conceived
this project and has been deeply committed to its success.

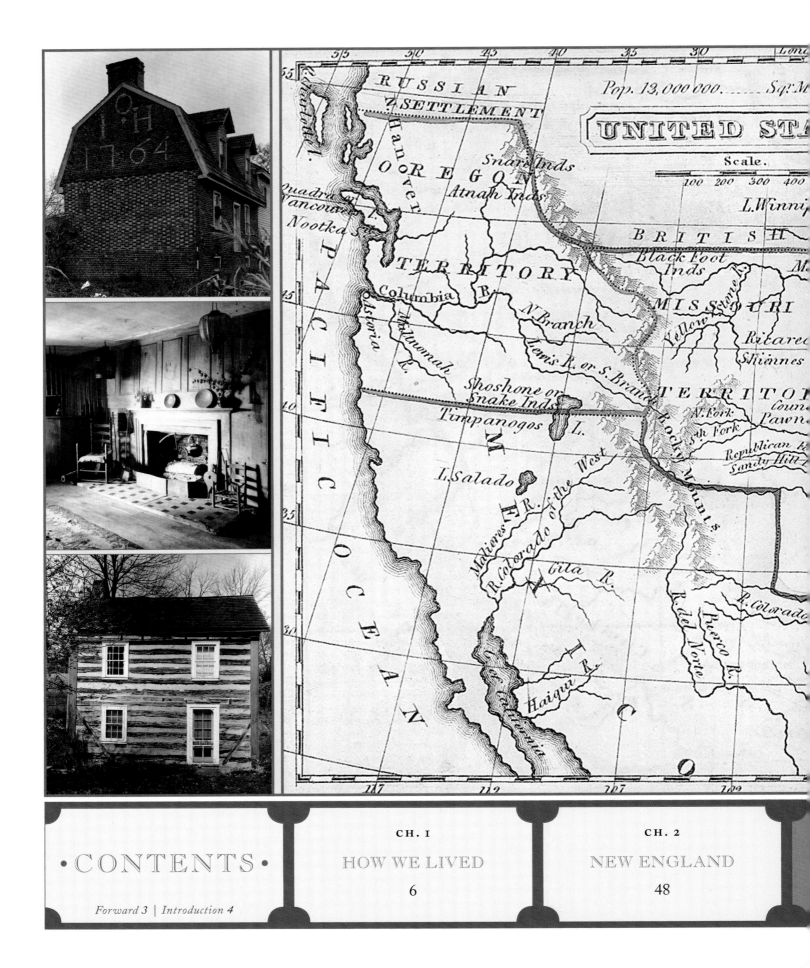

Distances from Washington
Boston . . . . 436 Miles
N. York 227
Philadelphia 137
Charleston 544
N. Orleans 1260
St. Louis 879
Vandalia 808
Columbus 418

FOREWORD

By Richard Moe
President, National Trust for Historic Preservation

This book is an engaging and eye-opening celebration of two great American treasures.

One is the marvelous collection of photographs and drawings produced under the auspices of the Historic American Buildings Survey. Launched during the Depression as a means of providing employment for out-of-work architects and photographers and still going strong today, HABS has compiled an invaluable and ever-growing archive of thousands of photos and drawings of American buildings – many of which, sadly, now exist only in these images. Fortunately for us, HABS photographers have always had a wide-ranging view of what's worth recording, capturing with equal thoughtfulness the elegant spire of a New England meetinghouse, the white-columned grandeur of a Mississippi mansion and the rust-pitted surface of a New Jersey door-latch. The result, as the pages of this book clearly demonstrate, is a treasure-trove of richly informative images – and a powerful testament to the skill and vision of those who created them.

The other treasure celebrated in these pages is the American house. Almost a century after the most recent of the structures depicted in Where We Lived was built, the famed modernist LeCorbusier said that a house should be "a machine for living in." Jack Larkin shows us how that machine worked in early America and how its owners tinkered with it to make it work better – as well as how they designed and decorated it to perpetuate traditional building practices, proclaim their status in the community… and, perhaps, impress their neighbors.

In a journey that spans the infant nation from New England to the Deep South, we see the full spectrum of early domestic architecture in all its quirky, graceful, crude, sophisticated, innovative, unabashed American-ness – and what a gloriously colorful spectrum it is.

From urban row houses and taverns to barns and privies, these places – many of them grand, others crumbling into ruin even then – open a window into the minds and lives of their builders. They remind us that a hugely important part of our nation's story is told in the houses that ornament our communities and shape and shelter our daily lives. More important, they inspire us to make sure that this heritage is kept intact and alive so that future generations can live with it, learn from it and draw inspiration from it – just as we do.

INTRODUCTION

A JOURNEY THROUGH A VANISHED LANDSCAPE

Like people, houses are created, live, and grow old. Like us, they eventually disappear. Houses that survive to be studied, explored, and admired by distant generations should be regarded as emissaries from another time, as gateways into our past.

In *Where We Lived*, these houses are our guides as we journey through the vanished landscape of our country when it was very young. Mile markers on this journey are the remarkable photographs of the Historic American Buildings Survey (HABS), created to document the nation's early structures.

The Survey had its origins in a time of national crisis. It began in 1933 as a program to find meaningful work for thousands of architects and draftsmen left unemployed when the Great Depression virtually brought construction in America to a halt. From 1934 to 1940, architectural survey teams documented thousands of houses, public buildings, and other structures, dating from the early 1600s through the mid-1800s. Many of the houses they documented, weakened even then, have not survived to our time.

Working out of offices in each state, HABS surveyors produced thousands of measured drawings, short histories of many buildings, and hundreds of thousands of photographs. Reborn on a smaller scale after World War II and more recently revitalized, the Survey has recorded more than 35,000 structures, creating a little-known treasury of American culture. Most of these black-and-white images are striking and evocative; some are starkly beautiful. They offer us a path to understanding the intertwined stories of early American families and their houses. Equally important, these photographs are crucial documents linking us to the past, as important in their way as our own family photographs.

Looking at these images reminds us that houses are familiar but also often mysterious. Old houses seem full of something glimpsed but not completely knowable—the everyday life and tangled family emotions of the past. We know that houses are not just wood and brick, plaster and glass. They are the physical settings for our deepest memories and strongest attachments, and they resonate with powerful emotions. In the past, houses were places not only in which to live but also to be born, to fall ill, to be cared for, and to die. A family living together was a household—a group of people held together, contained, and shaped by their dwelling place. Houses have lost some of these roles today, but they still shape our experiences of self and family. "Home, sweet home" may not always have been sweet, but it has always been important.

Most of us remember the details of our earliest home—rooms, doorways, windows and views, furnishings—imprinted on us in childhood. Many of us could jot down a floor plan from memory. Yet few of us ever record these memories. So neither did most of our early American counterparts. Such things were too ordinary to be worth describing or too intimate to be expressed. Much of what we know about life in early American houses and their surroundings comes from outside observers—travelers in a strange land who marveled, or were shocked, at what they saw and described it in letters and journals.

On this journey, we reimagine what houses meant to individuals and families in early America, from great mansions to tiny cabins: How did they work as "machines for living"? How did houses signal their owners' wealth and power? Respectability and aspiration? Comfort and independence? Survival? Powerlessness, poverty, and bondage? What did they look like, feel like, smell like? What compelling stories do they hold, and what significance do these houses and their stories have for us today? What so strongly connects us to them and our lives to those of our ancestors who were sheltered by these old houses?

The narrative of our journey draws heavily on travelers' accounts. Our first eyewitness speaks to us from 1775—Edward Parry, who kept a journal of his stay in Massachusetts at the very beginning of the American Revolution. It also relies on many other sources, including public records, community and family histories, letters and diaries, even novels and stories. It also takes note of a much earlier and almost forgotten Federal survey of buildings, the Direct Tax of 1798, which counted and measured houses from Maine to Georgia and today remains the only census of American houses ever taken.

Still, our story isn't a chronology of architectural development but an exploration. It moves across time and places to weave together stories of regions, ways of life, houses, and families. It begins with a look at the common features of home life—size and scale, space, crowding, privacy, cleanliness, everyday life.

Our journey follows the path taken by many early visitors to America: It starts in New England, moves to the Middle States, then to the South, and finally to what was the West—new states and the territories between the Appalachians and the Mississippi River.

Although the houses you see range from the earliest surviving homes of the New World to the "new" houses of the Greek Revival, the period we visit is that of the very young United States. It includes houses built as late as the early 1840s but goes no further. By that time, a radically new way of building houses—balloon framing—was emerging, a technology that would sweep traditional modes of construction. So here we draw the line.

Also at that time, the transforming power of the railroad and the factory, and the growth of great cities, were already at work to create a very different society. Its houses and families would be the subject of another book and another journey of exploration.

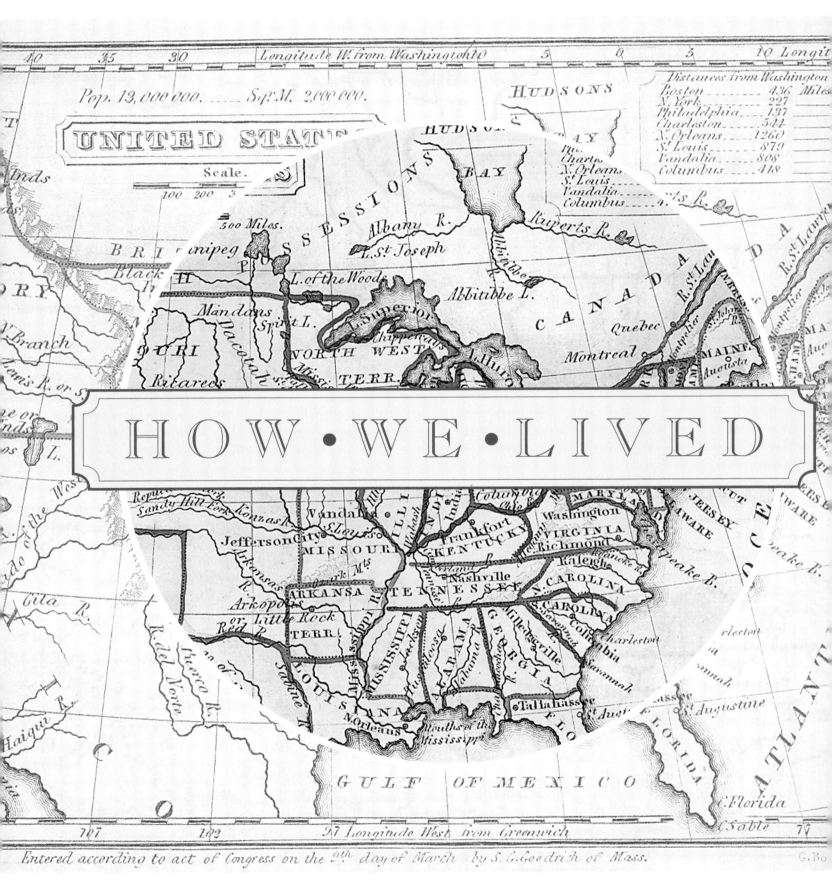

HOW · WE · LIVED

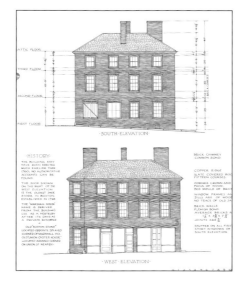

TRAPPED IN AMERICA

In letters, diaries, and journals kept to record events or ease boredom, many travelers—English, Scottish, French, and occasionally German, even wandering Americans—wrote about the people they came across, their habits, and the houses and taverns encountered on the way.

But none stayed so long and few reported so fully, so energetically, so disapprovingly, as Edward Parry, a well-connected Englishman who had spent his last two years as a "mast agent," surveying America's forests for the tall Eastern white pine that made the best masts for Royal Navy warships.

In 1775, Parry found himself trapped—first in rebellious Massachusetts and then, to his shock and dismay, in a typically cramped American farmhouse. It happened like this: He was on business in Georgetown, Maine, when local authorities seized him as a potential spy, dragged him to Boston, and turned him over to the Massachusetts legislature. Although he worked for the Royal Navy, Parry was a civilian so he couldn't be jailed as a prisoner of war. But he needed to have an eye kept on him in some remote location, a backwater where he couldn't observe sensitive activities or interfere with the war effort.

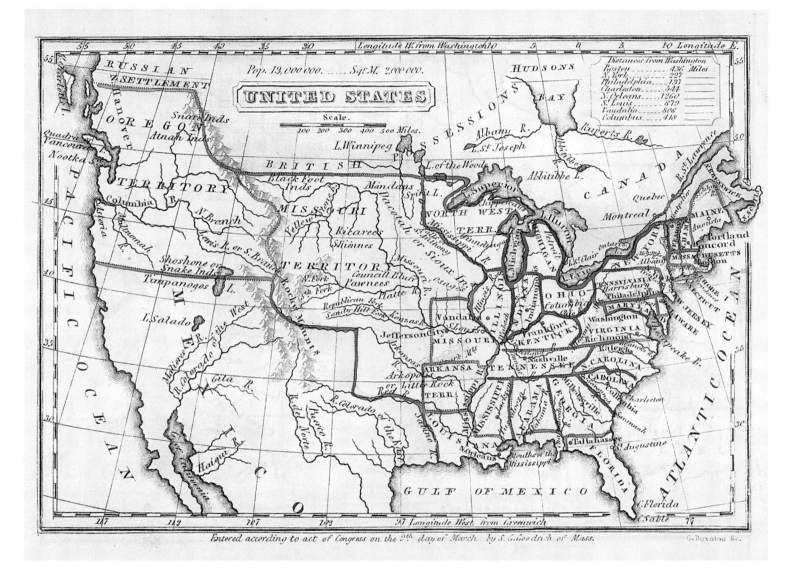

(above) The parlor floor of the
Leavitt house in this early
19th-century work is painted
with squares of brown and ocher,
just as Edward Parry described
Timothy Parker's best room. Joseph
Leavitt, "Interior of the Leavitt
Tavern" 1824, Chicestester, NH.

(right) The kitchen in the
1636 Fairbanks home in
Dedham, Massachusetts,
included the large fireplace
with beehive oven to its left
and would have contained a
table, a couple of chairs, and
some cooking pots. Although
it might look authentic, rifles
would not have hung over
the roaring fireplace, given
that the heat could have
ignited the gunpowder.

Parry's deeply unflattering portrait of the Parker household would have bewildered the Captain, who treated Parry more like a guest of honor than a prisoner. Yet, Parry felt bored and isolated. Compared with London, Boston, or even Portsmouth, Sturbridge was a "very lonely" place with not so much as a "public Road of any consequence thro' it." With little else to do, Parry threw his energies into his detailed and critical description of Sturbridge, the Parkers, their household and its daily routines, and everything else that annoyed him about his new life in exile.

CROWDING AND DISCOMFORT

A fastidious younger son of the English gentry, Parry found the house "a very miserable one," a single story with four rooms, two on either side of a central chimney, and above it a garret reached by a narrow staircase. Parry left no sketch of the house, but by his description it was probably a Cape Cod-style house, to this day one of New England's most characteristic houses.

At the front of the house was "the bed Room of the Representative, his wife and five small children, in which we breakfasted, dined and supped," Parry wrote. On the other side of the entryway was a space "called the best Room," which boasted the house's greatest effort at decoration: a tall case clock in one corner, a small cupboard built into another, and a floor painted with squares of "Spanish brown and Oker."

Captain Parker's best room was officially used "only on extraordinary occasions, when the Minister of the Parish or some other important person visited." The best room was intended to impress visitors with a display of the Parkers' best possessions. Many American families still treat their living room the same way.

On the back side of the house was a narrow kitchen about 10 ft. wide running most of the length of the house. Here the Parkers preserved food, cooked, made butter and cheese, and spun flax and wool. Next to the kitchen was "a small bed Room of 10 feet by 7" (smaller than a walk-in closets in a modern American "McMansion"). Although this space led into the best room, its door was always shut when visitors were in the house, just like we would shut the door on a messy kitchen when guests are over.

When Parry arrived, this house of only about 700 sq. ft. already had 12 people in it: the Captain and his wife, five young children, two hired girls (Parry described them as "dirty female servants"), and three laborers on the farm, one of whom was "a Negro man." (He might have been a slave, although Parry doesn't say. Slavery would not be abolished in Massachusetts until 1783.) The hired men and women all slept in the unfinished, uninsulated, and unventilated garret. The garret had no interior walls, although a blanket was probably hung across the center to separate the sexes.

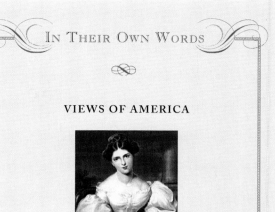

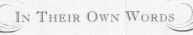

MARGARET HALL, INTREPID TRAVELER—AND CRITIC

Margaret Hunter Hall was not easy to please. She and her husband, British Navy Captain Basil Hall, took a two-year trip through the United States in 1828–29. Captain Hall went looking for information about the new country's government and laws, which he decided he disliked.

Margaret Hall did something much harder. She traveled the length of the United States with her toddler daughter Eliza and her maid. Mostly by stagecoach, they went from Boston to New Orleans and then back to New York. Somehow they all stayed "in perfect health," through New England snows, Philadelphia rain, and the torrid heat of the Gulf Coast.

Where Captain Hall noticed politics, Mrs. Hall noticed furniture, food, table manners, and houses. She put her observations into long letters to her sister back home but never dreamed of publishing them. Her letters didn't see print for a hundred years. If they had been published at the time, they would have caused more of a stir among touchy Americans than her husband's attacks on the follies of democracy. She noticed dirt in parlors, bedbugs in beds, lice on children's hair, and women's gowns dirtied by men's "incessant tobacco chewing."

Befitting his status as both guest and English gentleman, Parry himself had the small space off the best room "appropriated to my use, as a room solely for my purpose."

Used to the houses of the English aristocracy that were five to ten times larger, Parry found being the 13th member of the already packed Parker household trying. His journal notes Parry's dismay at finding the seven Parkers sleeping in one room, a space that would have contained three, maybe even four, beds. Here the Parkers not only slept and continued procreating, but at breakfast, lunch, and supper entertained ordinary guests and talked around the fire—all in full view of Captain and Mrs. Parker's "best bed" and the children's lesser beds. This tiny house was packed full of people night and day.

HARD WORK AND STRONG SMELLS

Parry found that the requirements of household work and storage intruded everywhere. Although the best room was set aside for special occasions, the rest of the time it held whatever the household was producing at a given time and used to store "milk pans, baked apples, and rough dry cloaths." Spinning wheels hummed in the kitchen, and the loom on which the women wove the family's woolen and linen cloth "was fixed in the loft or Garret over my Head."

At night the hired men and girls had to arrange their bedding around the heavy, virtually immovable loom; during the day the constant thumping of its shuttle and harnesses rumbled and shook the house.

Parry's own small room "was decorated in front with all the Stockings of the Family not in use—hanging upon a line—on the other side, hung a number of sundry Petticoats, Gowns, Female shoes." Along another wall "of my Bedchamber was hung—the industry of the Family being all the Skeins of Yarn, & linnen for the next weaving." But this wasn't all. In yet "another part of my bedchamber, hung a great many strings of dried Apples; it being the best part of the House for preserving them."

Then there were the smells: unwashed bodies and manure-stained boots and clothes. The fragrance of dried apples mixed with wood smoke, pipe tobacco, slightly souring milk, and ripening cheese. And finally, "in a corner of the Room lay an Indigo dye Pot filled with Chamber lye," a foul-smelling alkaline solution made from the concentrated leavings of the household's chamber pots. Its stench was "a constant perfume" that wafted through the house.

For meals, the Parker household crammed into the keeping room, pushing aside the beds to make room around the table that was covered by a stained tablecloth and set with "black and dirty" knives and forks that were "never Scoured, seldom whetted, and sometimes Washed." The "Negro man" ate by himself in the kitchen, the children were fed next "to prevent their Cryings," and the rest sat down to a meal presided over by Captain and Mrs. Parker, with the women on one side and the men on the other. The meal was usually "boil'd in one pot together . . . brot to table upon one dish" and served with hard cider that was passed around in a single grime-encrusted pewter pot.

Most unpleasant for Parry was a custom that was a matter of course to his hosts but deeply offensive to him. "Capt Parker," he confided to his journal, "requested me to suffer such persons as occasionally came into his house to partake of my bed." Two men sharing one bed was common. Parry's bed was probably the only one in the house that wasn't occupied by at least two people. The crowning indignity came on the night he was asked to share his bed with a social inferior, a traveling shoemaker.

Parry escaped from the Parker house after striking up a friendship with Joshua Paine, the town's Congregational minister. Paine had been educated at Harvard and grown up in a well-to-do merchant family near Boston. To his delight, Parry discovered that Paine lived much more like a gentleman than did the other men in town. After Paine smoothed the way with Captain Parker, Parry took up new accommodations. To the Englishman, Paine's house was a solitary oasis of civilization. For his part, Paine enjoyed Parry's gentlemanly manners and informed conversation.

Joshua Paine's house was considerably larger and his family smaller. Parry was given a room completely his own. His new setting offered "a tranquil and regular family," he wrote, "every thing neat and clean." It was "far above the Country Mediocrity" that he had found everywhere else. Strikingly, Parry didn't bother to describe the Paine house. It resembled, in a modest way, the houses he knew.

ASSESSING THE COUNTRY'S HOUSES

Parry left for England with unpleasant memories of his stay, but he might have done a lot worse in the broader context of American life of that time, whether in Pennsylvania, the rural South, or the rough frontier West. Another revealing source, the Federal Direct Tax of 1798, helps us understand this.

Much of what we know about the size and value of houses in early America comes from this remarkable set of documents, created as a revenue-raising measure during that year of political uncertainty and

(top) The loft of this mid-17th-century Virginia house in Appomattox has a board partition that might well have divided the men's sleeping space from the women's.

(bottom) This page from a Massachusetts assessor's log during the 1798 Direct Tax assessment records square feet, number of stories, number of windows, and "materials built of."

A lovely example of the Federal style of architecture from the beginning of the 1800s, this reflects fortunes that were made in the Massachusetts port city of Salem, renowned for its shipbuilding and trade with the Orient. Dodge-Shreve House, Salem, MA.

threats of war. To expand the Navy and other defense preparations, Congress levied a tax on all land, slaves, and houses in every state. Houses were the most important part of this tax scheme because, as Congressman Harrison Gray Otis of Massachusetts said, "nothing was a better or more certain sign of property than the house a man lives in." The tax forms required that houses be described in detail as to materials, number of stories, dimensions, and number of windows.

Between October and December 1798, a couple of thousand temporary Federal officials from Maine to Georgia went everywhere, inspecting houses and barns, referring to old tax lists, counting windows, arguing with suspicious homeowners. They added value for fanlights, pediments, and pilasters. They subtracted for broken windows and rotted clapboards.

The result was both a political disaster and a revelation. All over the country people resisted the tax. It was so unpopular that it helped sweep out the old Congress—along with President John Adams—and sweep in Thomas Jefferson and his supporters. Its value came much later, when people realized that the Direct Tax records provided the first—and except for recent census sampling—the only nationwide census of America's houses.

BIRDHOUSES

The smallest houses that Americans built were for birds. Benjamin Coe drew a number of houses in New England that had small dovecotes on their roofs or birdhouses on poles in the yard, and Margaret McVickar Grant remembered the unusual ones she saw around Albany, New York, in the 1790s. African-American workers (still enslaved) on large Hudson Valley estates drew on their own traditions to embellish their surroundings.

Every summer they made birdhouses "of every old hat that they could lay their hands on," by cutting holes in them and nailing them to the outside walls of their quarters. Grant sometimes counted "thirty or forty of these odd little domiciles, with the inhabitants busily going out and in." More surprisingly, they also made birdhouses out of the skulls of horses and cattle, attaching them to fences around gardens and cattle yards.

Slaves in the South, said Henry Cogswell Knight in 1817, made their own birdhouses near the quarters by putting up a tall pole and hanging hollow gourds around the top. Closer to the big house, the owners of large plantations fancied birds as well. They often built large, elaborate structures for songbirds and pigeons.

Slaves on a Virginia plantation probably built this elegant brick birdhouse. Chatham, Stafford County, Virginia.

On the Shetucket.

Birds fly overhead, roost on the roof, and roost in the birdhouses affixed to the gable end of this odd-looking house in Benjamin Coe's drawing of a "birdhouse" house on the Shetucket River in Connecticut. Courtesy of Old Sturbridge Village.

(top) This great house, named Drayton Hall, stood at the center of a thousand-acre plantation outside of Charleston, South Carolina, whose hundreds of slaves sustained the Drayton family's style of life. Visitors came from the entry hall into this room (bottom) to view a striking display of wealth and power in its expansive size, elaborate paneling, and intricate mantel.

Like many such documents, the schedules have survived piecemeal. Pennsylvania, Maryland, Massachusetts, and Maine have quite a few records. Fragments survive for New Jersey, New York, Vermont, New Hampshire, South Carolina, and Georgia. Taken together, they are complete enough to give a wide-ranging view of houses in the new America. As a whole, they show that just a few houses were at the top, a larger group just below, and most in the middle and bottom.

The great houses of America, "the standard of opulence" in the words of the men who designed the survey, were a few hundred houses like Drayton Hall outside Charleston, South Carolina, Mount Airy in Virginia, and the Dodge House in Salem, Massachusetts. These had three stories, a dozen or even 15 rooms, and many outbuildings and service wings. On the tax schedules they measured out at 3,000 sq. ft. or more and had 40 to 50 windows. Such houses were built to display the wealth and power of the greatest slaveholding planters or the success of merchants who had made fortunes in overseas trade. At the then-prevailing price level, they were valued at $10,000 or more. (An equivalent sum today might be $5 million.) Each would have been worth more than the total value of all the houses in many small communities.

Next came the houses of the gentry, successful merchants and lawyers, a few thousand "mansion houses" owned by maybe one family in a hundred. Less opulent than the greatest houses but still impressive, these might have 30 windows and measure at 2,000 sq. ft. Joshua Paine's residence was one of these.

These elite residences were the most likely to survive. Of most houses from the past, we're most likely to know these houses today. But these were vastly outnumbered by smaller houses. There were many thousands of sizable, comfortable homes for the prosperous—with perhaps 1,000 to 1,500 sq. ft. and 20 windows. There were many tens of thousands of modest houses like Timothy Parker's, with 600 to 1,000 sq. ft. and 10 to 15 windows. (Parker's house was assessed in 1798 at $270 and might have been called "decent" or "common" by American observers.) And making up the bulk of America's houses were the hundreds of thousands of tiny homes, ranging from 500 sq. ft. down to 200 sq. ft. or even less. At the time, others might have called them "mean" or "very ordinary."

Across the nation as a whole, about one-third of all the houses from 1798 were valued at less than $100, meaning that they weren't valuable enough to tax. Assessors sometimes added comments, noting in one case that a house was "poor and old" or another "very poor." Occasionally they struck a note of disbelief as in the comment, "one building called a house."

At the very bottom of the scale were the many thousands of tiny houses that tax assessors didn't even look at, the cabins and huts of slaves, who were a full one-sixth of the population. Although they are missing from the tax lists, other evidence, including the photographs in this book, assures us that they were as small and "mean" as the houses of the very poorest free Americans, crowded one-room houses with minimal furniture.

This "double house" in Kent County, Delaware, had fallen into serious disrepair by the time a HABS photographer shot it in 1936. But such neglect was not new. Many houses were described in the 1798 list with notes on their dilapidated condition, such as "a poor old house" or "much damaged."

IN THE WORDS OF TRAVELERS

Travelers left us with some amazing descriptions of houses at the very bottom of the social order. Sarah Kemble Knight encountered one in 1704. While trying to cross the Paukataug River in Rhode Island, she came upon a small house that housed a man, wife, and two children, and declared it "one of the wretchedest I ever saw habitation for human creatures."

The house was an "earth-fast" house, with no foundation, and its floor the bare earth. It had no windows, but the clapboards that enclosed it were "so much asunder, that the Light come throu' every where." The door was attached with a cord in place of hinges, and its only furniture was one bed for the whole family, "a Bord with sticks to stand on, instead of a table, and a block or two in the corner instead of chairs."

More than a century later, in 1831, James Stuart found another on the Illinois prairie. It was a small cabin "divided into three apartments by pieces of thin board and canvas, so that the blazing of the fire . . . afforded sufficient light for the whole of the house." There was not even a board to close up the house's one window opening. After getting into "the bedclothes of which I shall not attempt to describe," he found "on looking up, that the roof was more open than closed."

A ROOM BY ANY OTHER NAME

In one way or another, every house had space for sleeping, cooking, eating, working, sitting, and entertaining. But Americans used and named their rooms in a bewildering variety of ways. Even a quick look reveals regional differences, local variations, and idiosyncratic family preferences, as well as the inevitable drift of words' meanings over time.

One-room houses combined all their living functions in that single room. But while crowded, they usually weren't chaotic. Travelers testified that they were usually organized with invisible but clearly defined boundaries, delineating places for all the activities of living.

Two-room houses organized household space in terms of oppositions: public vs. private, outer vs. inner, work vs. sleeping. New Englanders in the 1600s spoke of hall and parlor, while Virginians used hall and chamber or great room and chamber. Germans in Pennsylvania used Stube and Kammer. Families cooked, did household work, and greeted visitors in the outer room. They slept in the inner one. Room names might change over time, but this fundamental pattern of organization persisted.

The least puzzling room names were those that had come into wide and general use. Americans mostly agreed that the room used for cooking was the kitchen (or German Koch), although in the South it was often a separate building. By 1800, a room set aside for sleeping was, in New England and the Middle States, usually called a bedroom if on the first floor of the house and a chamber or bedchamber if upstairs. Southerners still called downstairs rooms chambers. An unfinished space just below the roof and not always counted as a proper room was sometimes an attic, but often a garret in New England and a loft in the South.

(below) The years hadn't been kind to this East Greenwich, Rhode Island, house. The 1679 one-room portion of the larger house was actually the original building on the site, surviving many additions and expansions. It measures 19 ft. by 19 ft., or about 360 sq. ft., a reminder of the many one-room houses that were part of the landscape. Although the house looked doomed in this 1940 photograph, it was restored beginning later that year.

(facing page) This former slave cabin on the Will Crenshaw Plantation near Greenville, Alabama, built in the early 1800s, had two rooms, two doors, and a single gable-end chimney. It probably housed two families.

THE PLACE OF THE PARLOR

If the surveyors of 1798 had asked, they probably would have recorded that almost every house with three or more rooms had one space "set apart as its place of especial social hilarity and sanctity," as Harriet Beecher Stowe put it. This was the best room, devoted to entertaining. It was also called simply a hall, a great room, a Stube, and other names. By the early 1800s the word parlor was taking over, and by the mid-1800s it had taken over completely.

As material standards improved and houses became larger, the parlor changed again. As later generations acquired more furniture—chairs, chests, tables, dishes—they were what people wanted to show off. Beds had originally been the major "trophy"

(above) A beautifully monogrammed gable end declares this the home of William and Mary Oakford and the year of its construction on their behalf, 1736, in Salem County, New Jersey. The first floor held one 405-sq.-ft. room and the upstairs three tiny chambers.

(right and opposite) Built about 1750 in Berks County, Pennsylvania, this two-story house, built of logs and chinked with clay, measures a tiny 16 ft. by 20 ft. It has one room on the first floor and two small chambers separated by a thin partition on the second. Below them is a stone cellar with a large cooking fireplace. Probably the majority of American families lived in houses no larger.

HABS No. PA-258A-1

possession, but after 1800 or so, most families began to feel that a bed on display in the parlor was more of an embarrassment than a status symbol. Next, the parents' bed left the parlor for a first-floor bedroom or an upstairs chamber. And by 1820, parlor had come to mean a formal and often rarely used room for entertaining and displaying a family's best things. The parlor was no longer for sleeping.

In larger houses, the parlor or best room was paired with another space, called a "second-best room" often of identical size. (Edward Parry described such a pair of rooms in the Parker house.) With one room set aside strictly for formality, the other was for eating, family gatherings, informal visits, and light work such as sewing, knitting, reading, and writing. In Southern houses, this room was sometimes called the dining room. Everywhere else, it was the sitting room, the family parlor, or the back parlor.

Except in the biggest houses, it was rare to have a room set aside just for eating. Although Virginians spoke of the dining room, they used it as a multipurpose family space. Many families took most of their meals in the second-best room, removed a little from the messy kitchen.

HARDLY EVER USED

Although the parlor or best room was the most prominent room, foreigners were amazed, as Parry was in 1775, by how little use they saw. They were places, the English traveler John Abdy said in 1820, that witnessed only the "marriages of the living and the last rites of the dead." The "fashionable shut-up parlor was cold, uninviting and stately . . . devoid of human light or warmth," Stowe wrote.

The widely read *Housekeeper's Book* of 1837 wrote that most families had "show rooms" that were "considered too fine to be habitually occupied." When these parlors were opened on a rare occasion, children "would stare about them as if they had never beheld the place before." Americans later recalled how, as children, they dreaded the parlor. It was the "colder region" of the house, which offered only discomfort amid "high and slippery chairs with upright backs which . . . preached decorum."

Although critics abounded, Americans gave no hint of giving up the room. For them the parlor was no less important to home life than the kitchen. It helped define who they were in the world, even if they hardly ever used it. The tradition persists today. Although we don't use the word parlor, many of us still shut off a room from daily use. It's usually called the living room, even though living goes on elsewhere, usually in the family room and kitchen.

Built-in corner cupboards were a common feature of parlors, or best rooms, and provided a formal setting for the storage and, more important, the display of a family's best things. This parlor cupboard belongs to the Obadiah Smith House in Smithtown, New York, and dates to 1740.

THE ALL-IMPORTANT ENTRY

Entering a house in early America could happen one of two ways. You could simply open a front door and step into the middle of a family's daily routine. Or you would find yourself in an entryway, a threshold area between outside and inside.

Into the early 1800s, most American houses were what is called "socially open," so there wasn't a transition area, or entryway, between the front step and the daily living space. Only a single door, one that anyone could open, separated the house from the roadside, the household from the neighborhood. The boundary between the life of the family and the life of the community was easy to cross.

For a house to have an entryway marked an increased separation between the outside world and the family life inside. The family could compose itself to meet its guests or determine how they would be received.

The new Georgian architectural styles that first came to America in the early 1700s emphasized order, symmetry, and clear boundaries between inside and outside. They always included a hallway that straddled the line between outside and inside. Over time, a smaller proportion of socially open houses were built in America, but many thousands were still built every year.

This openness was inevitable in one-room and two-room houses, which were everywhere, and it remained the standard in smaller houses from Pennsylvania south. But in the rural North, in cities, and among the wealthy everywhere, a separate entry space had become a necessity by the early 1800s and a mark of respectability. To these families, the open door and the open house meant backwardness.

Of course, not all entryways were the same. They varied a great deal in size, impressiveness, and social function. Central-chimney houses, common in New England and in parts of New York, New Jersey, Pennsylvania, and Ohio, had small entryways that offered only enough room for a few people to stand before they were let in. These preserved some privacy and conserved heat in winter.

Built across America, central-hallway houses on the Georgian (later Federal) plan had an entry hall running the depth of the house, which provided larger and more imposing entry spaces. At its most impressive, the hallway of a great house was part of its presentation of wealth and power. Its scale asked visitors to look upwards. The doors to numerous rooms opened off from it and a staircase flowed gracefully up to the floors above. Visitors from smaller houses would be impressed, even awed. Social equals would recognize an appropriate reception. We might note another possibility as well. A visitor could be asked to wait, while members

Taking tea was an important social ritual for many American families after 1750 or so. For the most important visitors, it took place in the parlor; for more familiar ones, in the sitting room.

of the household remained behind closed doors and decided how, or whether even if, to receive a guest.

Using the front entryway of the "mansion house" and being allowed to experience its formal welcome honored the visitor. Then, as now, the back door or kitchen door had a different role. Among more ordinary families it was a mark of long, informal acquaintance. In larger houses it was a sign of social equality not with the owners but with children and the help.

BIG FAMILIES AND SMALL HOUSES
American families were big. Edward Parry counted 12 in Captain Parker's house, and that wasn't unusual.

(above) The small front entry on this 1730 New England house opens almost immediately onto the stairs to the second floor. To the right and the left are the doors to the parlor and sitting room of the house.

(right) A grand stair hall, with a dramatically centered stair swooping directly up to the second-floor gallery, provides a striking entrance to the circa 1800 McLellan-Sweat House in the small city of Portland, Maine.

The midwife introduces a new baby to a toddler while the father looks on. The mother is "lying-in" in a hung bed whose curtains are partially open. The engraving is from **Mother Goose's Pocket of Pleasure 1840.**

A house on the Featherstone tenant farm near Lowndesville, in South Carolina's Upper Savannah River region, began as a one-room log cabin, 19 ft. by 17 ft., in about 1800. A later frame addition, visible to the left, provided an extra room 12 ft. by 17 ft. Its fireplace and chimney were removed when the house was converted into a farm storage shed.

Married couples in the captain's town of Sturbridge averaged more than eight children per family.

Describing a pioneer farm in Kentucky around 1800, Daniel Drake wrote that "the usual large number of ragged children was at the door." Traveling on the north shore of Massachusetts at the same time, the Rev. Timothy Dwight saw "children everywhere . . . at every door a new flock." Several decades later, a New York merchant's wife wrote her sister that "we now lay . . . our table for thirteen persons daily."

During the 1700s the country's birth rate was among the highest in the world, and it remained high even as it slowly declined in the 1800s. In 1790, the new United States became the first nation to adopt a regular population census. The census for 1790 and 1800 showed that half of all households contained seven people or more. Large as this figure is, it underestimates the number of Americans living in large families. For some part of their childhood, most Americans lived in households of eight or nine people. Probably one

❀ EVERYDAY LIFE ❀

Peeling Away the Past

Historic houses often lie buried beneath the additions and alterations of contemporary homes. Well-meaning owners sometimes strip away these improvements to work their way back to the historic core—or to a guess at how the place once looked.

In the 1930s, an attractive home in Johnston, Rhode Island (far left), was shorn of everything believed to have been added to the one-room Thomas Clemence House (left), built around 1679. Today, historic preservationists might not sanction such a drastic treatment, sometimes preferring to maintain the integrity of a house as it has evolved over time.

American in six lived in a household of 13 or more. By comparison, our households today are tiny. The 2000 census shows that the average family size is 2.6.

Another reason so many people lived in a single house is that houses were the fundamental institution for taking care of people. The great majority of households were built around a husband and wife and their unmarried children but could include many others. A married couple might take in elderly parents, unmarried brothers and sisters, widowed daughters, and orphaned grandchildren—even married children and their kids.

Affluent country families had domestic workers, or "helps," and farm laborers. Craftsmen such as blacksmiths, cabinetmakers, and printers usually took in an apprentice or two, and often housed a journeyman employee as well. In cities and villages, less wealthy families took in paying boarders, usually young men working nearby and away from home.

In slaveholding houses, slaves sometimes outnumbered the family. For people to live by themselves (in a one-person household so common today) was almost unknown, and the relative handful of people who did were considered eccentric, outcast, even insane. With few alternatives such as hospitals, nursing homes, long-term-care and assisted-living facilities, apartment complexes, and other modern forms of shelter, houses and households were the primary source of shelter in a way not easy now for us to grasp.

LEARNING TO SHARE

Edward Parry felt oppressed living with 12 other people in a house with only four rooms, although his circumstances weren't that unusual. High birth rates meant that even big houses would become crowded as the number of children steadily mounted, particularly before the older ones left home. Only recently have we grown used to plenty of personal space. Our houses are larger and our families smaller than ever. Just as we can hardly imagine their world, they could not have imagined ours.

We can get a sense of just how crowded houses could be, however, by combining the 1798 house census with the 1800 population census for two small farming communities—the township of Lower Alloways Creek in New Jersey and the town of Brookfield, Massachusetts. The results are eye-opening. Brookfield houses averaged just over 120 sq. ft. per person. Lower Alloways houses had about 90 sq. ft. per person. In contrast, the Federal houses survey for 1999–2000 reported an average of 1,200 sq. ft. per person. Today we have 10 to 14 times more personal space than our ancestors had. Only a handful

Aspendale, near Kenton, Delaware, has eight rooms and was the main house of a mid-size Delaware plantation. Built between 1771 and 1773, the clay for the bricks used in the Georgian-style structure was dug from the property. Local legend holds that during the Revolutionary War lead from the roof was removed and used to make bullets.

of houses had anything close to "modern" amounts of space per person, and each of them was owned by a prosperous elderly couple with no children left at home.

CONSTANT TOGETHERNESS— EVEN IN BED

Parry's single bed and unshared room was a rarity and a privilege granted only guests. The reality was that few people slept alone. Infants slept with their parents; cradles were used only during the day. Small children slept three or four together. Family members had beds of their own only for serious illness or childbirth and recovery. An older brother or sister would share a bed with a toddler, who had been appointed his or her "assigned charge." Like most women, Susan Lesley remembered her "mother-sisters" with whom she "always slept, from the time of my infancy."

(above) The southeast chamber in this house, a space that would have been just for sleeping, is a small room with a steeply sloping ceiling. Although the kneewalls and ceiling in this loft space are plastered, they well might not have been for occupants who lived here in the 18th and early 19th centuries, though the windows would have been a welcome feature.

(right) The Thomas Gaddis House, built between 1769 and 1793, shows the simple corner winder stair that led to the second floor. Gaddis was locally famous as a leader of the 1794 Whiskey Rebellion, which was quashed when George Washington sent 15,000 troops to put it down.

Sleeping spaces were sparely furnished. "Farmers are not luxurious in their notions of these second-floor apartments," noted New York architect Andrew Jackson Downing in 1845. They were used "merely for the purpose of sleeping."

"At the head of the back stairs" as Harriet Beecher Stowe described a boys' bedchamber in a New England house, "was a rude little crib, roughly fenced off from the passageway by unplaned boards of different heights. A pine table, two stools, a small trundle bed, and a rude case of drawers, were all its furniture." Many chambers had less—no more than a bedstead and an old chair for hanging clothes.

In many a small house, children slept in the loft or garret on straw "ticks," scratchy mattresses without frames. Unmarried daughters shared not only bedchambers but beds with each other and with female servants. In large Northern farmhouses, laborers often shared a bed or two in the garret with the older boys. Those who grew up sleeping in the garret remembered the countless sharp shingle nails sticking through the roof's thin sheathing that

This traditional New England farmhouse in Acton, Massachusetts "of the better sort," as it would have been called it in its day, has eight rooms plus additions that have grown from the early 1700s to the early 1800s.

THOSE RIDICULOUS AMERICANS

In 1828, the Scottish Margaret Hunter Hall toured the United States with her two-year-old daughter, Eliza. From north to south, she sent back to her sister in England letters filled with frank impressions of Americans, their manners, and habits. This is from her description of a party in a fancy New York City home.

"When they come to light ballroom conversation nothing can be so ponderous, and, as for an attempt at a joke, the weight of it is enough to crush you to atoms. The women do not bear the test of evening dress. They have no air, and, tho' they have plenty of good clothes on, the taste is not good. There was too great a mixture of flowers and pearls and different kinds of ornaments in the hair. They hold themselves ill, I saw but one person who danced well."

would rip the clothes of anyone who came too close. In freezing weather, the nail heads would shine from frost accumulated from the sleepers' warm breath. P. T. Barnum remembered his younger brother's practical joke of sneaking into bed wearing boots and spurs during the years the two shared a bed with the family's succession of hired men.

CLOSE TOGETHER: A WAY OF LIFE

Early Americans had a different sense of privacy. For one thing, so much of their work in the field, kitchen, and shop was done alone. Crowding around a table for meals or sitting tightly side by side next to an evening fire was satisfying. For ordinary people, sharing rooms and beds was a necessity, even comforting. The young apprentice Edward Carpenter noted several times in his diary that he went "to find someone to sleep with" when the fellow lodger with whom he usually bunked was away overnight.

When the need arose, beds could be put almost anywhere in the home—kitchens, sitting rooms, and garrets. With family and friends gathered for a wedding on a Georgia plantation in 1829, Henry Worth remembered that every room was crowded with beds, with extra ticks laid on the floor and in the passageways.

English traveler Isaac Weld wrote in 1796 that "the people at the American farm houses will cheerfully lie three in a bed, rather than suffer a stranger to go away who comes to seek for lodging." Thirty years earlier, the Englishman Andrew Burnaby recounted even greater generosity in a way that's nearly unimaginable to modern sensibilities. In a tiny Pennsylvania house with only one bed, he "got into bed. After some time the old gentlewoman came to bed . . . after her the old gentleman, and last of all the young lady."

In rural Crawford County, Pennsylvania, as late as the 1820s, "it was not unusual when only one bed was had, for the good wife to put it on the floor, her husband in the middle, she on one side of him and the guest on the other," farmer John Reynolds recalled. "I have myself slept so in a neighbor's cabin." This "could only proceed from simplicity and innocence," Burnaby thought. It surely reflected a high level of tolerance for close physical contact with strangers.

True privacy of either sight or sound was not easy to come by indoors. In one- and two-room houses it was nearly impossible. Thin walls and loosely joined floorboards meant that much could be seen and heard. Witnesses testifying in court well into the 1800s frequently noted how easy it was to overhear conversations or peer into adjoining rooms, particularly in small houses.

In this early 19th-century woodcut, the mother spins flax in the kitchen while her daughter reads by firelight. Anecdotes for Children, N.Y., c 1840

WHEN A BED BECOMES A ROOM

In most households through the early 1800s, at least one bed, usually the parents', was "hung" or "enclosed tight with curtains hung from a frame, often fringed, tasseled and embroidered," as Charles Gorman of Pennsylvania described it in 1805. The elaborate curtains held in warmth during cold weather and, if they were nice enough, would be something to show off to visitors. And for the majority of couples who shared sleeping space with other members of the family, curtains provided a little bit of privacy.

After about 1820 bed curtains started to disappear. More parents had bedrooms of their own, and better heating made things a bit warmer. Also, the new French bedstead that had no curtains was much more elegant. At the same time, medical writers began promoting the health benefits of ventilation, warning that heavy bed hangings obstructed the airflow and allowed noxious vapors to accumulate. The new-style beds matched the recommendations of a New York physician who wrote in 1838 that beds "be freed as possible from unnecessary clothing, and everything which could retain bad air."

❖ EVERYDAY LIFE ❖

Artist of the Ordinary: Benjamin Coe

Benjamin Coe was an artist and drawing teacher in Connecticut and New York who never became famous. He published a couple

of small books in the 1840s, with examples of how to draw landscapes and houses. He wasn't interested in great mansions or romantic views, but took pleasure in drawing ordinary things.

He drew small houses in New York and Connecticut that few other artists would have cared about. He depicted everyday details such as rain barrels, gutters, and birdhouses. He also drew houses in poor repair, showing where clapboards were missing or shingles had come off the roof. Coe's drawings give us a look at the ordinary landscape of American life.

Privies, or outhouses, ran the gamut in size, shape, and quality of construction. This wood-frame Virginia privy (below) was built with raised-panel surrounds and multiple seats, giving it an elegant appearance. The brick privy found in Maryland (above), however, seems to ignore some basic boundaries of human behavior: It combines in one structure a privy with a smokehouse.

These reformers were a lot less successful when they tried to get Americans to stop sharing beds, although they tried. Prescribing individual privacy in the service of health, experts urged every "bed should contain only one person . . . and there should be but one bed" in a room. Some prosperous families with plenty of room were receptive to the idea. In their houses, mostly in New York and New England cities and villages, beds and bedchambers became individual possessions for all family members.

Andrew Jackson Downing noted that, among some well-to-do families, bedchambers were furnished "for the purpose of passing the time in elegant leisure," allowing occupants to go upstairs to read, sew, or take tea in warm weather. Two of America's greatest writers, Emily Dickinson and Henry Thoreau, were among the beneficiaries. Both lived as single adults in their parents' homes. Both famously kept to their own rooms and found the solitude they needed to write.

❊ EVERYDAY LIFE ❊

Necessary House

Well into the 19th century, indoor plumbing existed in only a tiny number of American houses. The chamber pot and the privy (or outhouse), with water hauled in from a well, spring, or creek, were the basics of sanitation for most of the country.

Many houses in thinly settled areas had no privies at all. Families simply used surrounding woods or bushes. An archeological study of one rural house site in the Northeast found no privy for the first several decades of the house's existence. But a look at an early barn foundation found a concentration of telltale chemical residues that reveals more about the family's life than they would have wanted us to know.

Privies came in different sizes. Some could be used by several people at once, and a few had interior paneling. Most were small "necessary houses" for one or two people, built with one important but rarely discussed function in mind.

NY.471-H

But for most American families, these recommendations were impossible to put into practice or even to comprehend, given the circumstances of their houses and life. Separate beds for everybody wouldn't be a widespread reality until the 20th century.

On a cold night, a bed hung with drapes like this one would have meant a better night's sleep in addition to a bit of privacy, given that four or five other people also might have been sleeping in the room. This is the Jean Hasbrouck House in New Paltz, New York.

RARELY CLEAN AND USUALLY SMELLY

Eternal grime and the odor of chamber pots were some of Edward Parry's strongest impressions of the Parker farmhouse. In a world before the introduction of outdoor plumbing, the sink, water bucket, chamber pot, and privy defined the boundaries of home sanitation.

No one in the Parker household, or anywhere else in the country for that matter, bathed regularly in the modern sense. "There was not the slightest sign of . . . ewers, lavers and basins, nor of pails and tubs" in the furnishings of bedchambers before 1800, wrote Alice

The Stencil House

Wallpaper and wooden paneling weren't the only ways to decorate a room. Stenciling—painting a repeating pattern directly on the wall using a stiff paper template—was another.

Around 1835, John Nunnely built a dogtrot-style log house in Clifton, Tennessee. Not long afterward, a traveling stencil artist passed through and decorated the walls. These stenciled decorations look a lot like the work of Moses Easton of New Hampshire, the best-known American stencil painter. But he doesn't seem to have strayed this far from home.

More likely, it was another artist, still anonymous, who was copying or borrowing Eaton's designs. Some other surviving houses in Tennessee, Indiana, and Illinois have similar stenciled walls. The "Stencil House" is still standing. To provide for its preservation, it has been moved from Clifton to the Ames Plantation in Grand Junction, Tennessee.

CONN-204-A.

CONN. S. BROOK, 4A-1

Morse Earle, one of the first historians of American everyday life. "This conspicuous absence speaks with a persistent and exceedingly disagreeable voice of the unwashed condition of our ancestors."

Bathing came to America in the 1790s when rich city families began to follow the practice of the British aristocracy. From Philadelphia, New York, and Boston, it spread to elite plantation houses in the South and then, over the course of a few decades, to "respectable" families in cities and villages. Those who took "a full cold bath every morning," as teacher and writer Lucy Larcom recalled, were part of a domestic revolution. Without the central heat and hot tap water that we take for granted, "it required both nerve and will to do this in a room without a fire." By the 1830s, the bedchambers of many houses boasted the washstands, basins, and pitchers that were signs of a new cleanness.

It took a few more decades before bathing became the norm for average Americans. In Northern farmhouses, Francis Underwood's family continued to go "down to the back sink-room" to wash only "our faces and hands" with cold water from a bucket. Instead of soap they used "a brisk rub on a coarse rolling-towel." In the South, Scottish traveler James Stuart noted in 1833 that people washed not in their houses but outside, "at the

EVERYDAY LIFE

A Better Way to Go

A commode was a more decorous way of using a basic chamber pot. It was called a commode because it would have been more commodious, or helpful, to the user. A commode such as this one would have been especially helpful for an elderly person or an invalid.

Although it wasn't really necessary to have a commode, many people who bought and used them saw it as a more refined or genteel way to take care of those basic bodily functions. Hiding the chamber pot in a commode also provided a bit more comfort and propriety. And it also kept the chamber pot out of sight and somewhat out of the sensory range of people in the house.

In 1800, a cabinetmaker would have made a customer a commode such as this one for two or three dollars, though probably no more than five, this in a time when such a craftsman might have earned about a dollar a day. *Courtesy of Old Sturbridge Village.*

ALA., 49. CHAST, 1-1   HABS

Built about 1830 near Mobile, Alabama, the Zeno Chestang dogtrot house is raised on piers to keep the house dry during high water. The passage, or dogtrot, through the center allowed better airflow during the hot, humid summer weather near the Gulf Coast.

vermin with which I was molested." In 1828, Joseph Fowler, another Englishman, found them in New York City, Albany, Rochester, and in every village in between.

That same year, on a trip from Maryland to Louisiana, the Scotswoman Margaret Hall found infested beds, dirty underclothing, and heads "absolutely crawling" with lice. Charles Dickens wryly noted finding "a kind of game not on the bill of fare" while on his American tour in 1841. Farm periodicals provided recipes for ridding beds of vermin. And the *Farmer's Almanac,* New England's agricultural bible, excoriated wives who "let a tired farmer be tormented all night."

In warm weather, empty fireplaces were "a free entrance into the house" for swarms of bugs, birds, and bats, as German traveler Peter Kalm observed in 1748 Pennsylvania. The solution was to close up fireplaces with wooden fireboards, which usually were painted with scenes. However, neither blinds nor fireboards could keep out the mosquitoes, which plagued everybody. Kalm wrote how they would "approach nearer and nearer to the bed, and at last suck up so much blood that they can hardly fly away."

By the late 1820s, advocates for better housekeeping practice were urging the use of window screens of cloth netting or even more expensive wire mesh. Only a few households could follow this costly advice. Houseflies in the kitchen and mosquitoes in the bedchamber remained a constant torment.

Flies also added to the general filth of houses, which in summertime had flyspecks everywhere, on furniture, walls, curtains. Without screens, keeping bugs out of the kitchen and dairy room was next to impossible. Keeping farmhouses tidy with broom, bucket, and mop was a losing battle because dirt and grime came in from everywhere—fields, barnyards and pigsties, muddy or dusty roads, open windows, fireplaces. Add to the battle against filth all the other household duties, like cooking, preserving food, making butter and cheese, sewing and mending, and caring for the children, and you get a sense of how unmanageable housekeeping might have seemed to a woman of the time.

In 1770 Mary Cooper of Oyster Bay, New York, confided to her diary that despite all her work both she and her house were "dirty and distrest." Housekeeping was easier for women who didn't have farm responsibilities or who had plenty of help. Big plantation houses down South had no shortage of domestic labor, but they ran the gamut of domestic order and disorder. In Margaret Hall's assessment, the planters' houses she visited in South Carolina ranged from a few where "everything looked so clean and comfortable" to those where "all was dirty and nasty."

Filth and slovenliness were everywhere else, too. The aisles of churches and meetinghouses would be fouled by dogs and chickens that wandered in and out in warm weather. Men in church, even those in the choir, chewed and spat tobacco, and families littered their pews with nutshells and apple cores. Not only taverns but also courthouses and legislatures were filthy and spattered with tobacco juice. Schoolhouses were frequently unswept, strewn with refuse from pupils' lunches, and bedaubed with ink.

LIFE WAS DARK, CLOSE, AND STILL

Edward Parry valued the little window in his room because it allowed him to cool off in summer when the kitchen fire roared and because there wasn't much other light. The darkness of night, or even a cloudy day, wasn't easy to overcome. In her autobiography, *A New England Girlhood*, Lucy Larcom remembered "primitive ways of doing things." For light, "we used tallow candles . . . and sat by open fireplaces."

WHAT'S WRONG WITH AMERICAN HOUSES?

Theodore Dwight, the grandson of Timothy Dwight, took his own tour through the United States in 1828. He was not impressed with how his fellow Americans organized and furnished their houses. "Some of our countrymen," he said, "believe that there is no architectural taste independent of red, green, or blue paint," which they splashed on to make their houses fashionable or at least visible.

But much worse, he thought, were houses that were designed only for the "hollow and ruinous ceremonies of fashionable life" and neglected the needs of the family. Houses were first of all places for raising children. Dwight thought that he was invoking the virtuous past, but in reality, he was expressing a new idea. Previous generations had thought that houses were primarily places for adults, in which children's needs hardly had to be considered.

Dwight urged American families to reduce the physical scale of domestic life; they should "contract the walls and depress the ceilings of our houses to a reasonable size." Along with smaller houses would go bigger moral and intellectual ambitions. Giving up "spacious and gaudy apartments . . . frivolous morning calls . . . and nightly dancers," they would teach their children and gather the household around the fireside as their ancestors had.

Needless to say, few Americans heeded this advice. They went on building ever larger houses and displaying their status through architecture.

Making candles from beef fat was repetitive drudgery that spanned two or three days in November or December.

Women in prosperous farm families made 40 to 50 dozen candles a year, enough to keep a big house fairly well lit by standards of the time. Poorer farmers who didn't slaughter beef annually had to buy or trade for tallow and could not always afford enough candles to light the house at night. Most country households had a pair or two of candlesticks—made of brass, pewter, or iron and usually kept in the kitchen when they weren't being used. Some might have a dozen or more, along with the luxury of all that light. For others, "for want of a better," wrote a newspaper editor about candlesticks in 1835, "I have seen one made out of a piece of board and nails, and even out of a turnip or a potato."

Yet even with plenty of candles the world was dim. A single candle (equivalent to a five-watt bulb) "cut but a small circle into the darkness" of a room at night, Harriet Beecher Stowe wrote, and left "all the rest of the apartment in shadow." Except on sunny days, Americans coped with indoor light levels that we would find very uncomfortable. Tasks like sewing and reading followed the morning and afternoon sun around the house.

GETTING MORE LIGHT

After 1810 or so, people who lived in cities and villages began replacing or supplementing candles with whale oil lamps, which shed light equal to several candles. More impressive were Argand-style lamps (available after 1820) that burned expensive, highly refined sperm whale oil and were brighter than 20 candles. People were starting to create brighter nighttimes than ever before known. For most rural families, though, candles remained the light source. The new Argand lamps cost more than candlesticks, and lamp oil, unlike tallow, couldn't be made on the farm.

Because all light came from open flame, all light was potentially hazardous. Candles would tip over and set things afire. Susan Blunt recalled a neighbor who when "reading the newspaper . . . held the candle so close to the paper that he set it on fire." The liquid fuel of oil lamps made them even more dangerous when one was knocked over. Vigilance was necessary as long as any light was burning. A sleeping household was always in complete darkness.

The poorest families—slaves, city laborers, tenant farmers—often had only the fireplace for light. In 1824 a Scottish traveler named Patrick Shireff visited a "poor habitation" on the Illinois frontier that was "lighted by what they termed a string, or piece of twine, dipped in tallow, and which gave a glimmering light, so that we could scarcely distinguish objects."

SUNLIGHT AS A STATUS SYMBOL

Windows were counted in the 1798 Direct Tax schedules not because glass was highly expensive—in fact, it was becoming steadily less costly—but because daylight was both practically and symbolically important. Windows not only provided illumination but also were a good measure of comfort and prosperity. The number and size of windows varied a great deal. The poorest houses recorded by the Direct Tax had one, two, or three windows, usually very small. The greatest houses had upwards of 60, often amounting to more than 1,000 sq. ft. of glass.

(above) In the summertime, these shutters would have been all that stood between the indoors and the out, although insects certainly would have found their way through the louvers. The first-floor window belongs to Wright Tavern in Concord, Massachusetts, where on the night of April 18, 1775, committee members of the colony's Provincial Congress met to discuss the pending war, which broke out the next day.

(right) This parlor setting would have caught any visitor's eye with its overmantel painting. Covering the fireplace is a decorated fireboard that would have kept out dirt, birds, and swarms of insects during the summer.

(above) Bucks County, Pennsylvania, is famous for its stone houses and for its Quaker communities. This center-hall stone English Quaker house, a near perfect example of its type, was built in 1812 by the Foulke Family of Quakertown, Pennsylvania.

(right) Holding a lighted candle, a mother takes her two girls up to bed. The woodcut emphasizes the small islands of candlelight that shone in the darkness of the house. The Rose Bush, c. 1840.

The trend began in the mid-1700s with the Georgian style of architecture. A symmetrical façade with plenty of well-made windows let everybody see that here was a home of taste and prosperity. Passersby could count windows to estimate the number of rooms in the house and how much it had cost. Especially large windows could even be seen as a sign of arrogance, as the Rev. Ebenezer Parkman discovered. In 1751 he built a house with 13 large windows. He was pleased with his display of taste and prosperity until a prominent member of his congregation took him to task about "the pride of Ministers, when he saw the Window Frames." He went on to write in his diary that he was now sorry that "the windows were so large."

In summer, large windows provided too much light and heat, so better houses had exterior blinds or shutters that allowed air to circulate while keeping out too much sunlight. Many houses were kept wholly or partially shuttered all summer. If the shutters were painted the same color as the rest of the house, travelers often noted an appearance from afar of a house having no windows at all.

A WORLD OF STARK LIMITATIONS

From cleanliness and domestic sanitation to pest control, lighting, and heat, the early Americans whose houses you see here shared the stark limitations of a time before indoor plumbing, central heating, and most other forms of what's now considered basic technology. Their houses were usually crowded with people, and their notions about privacy were a world apart from ours. They lived in inequality no less visible than in our own society, in conditions ranging from ragged discomfort to elegance and ease.

Yet their houses also reveal an enormous and fascinating diversity. From Maine to Louisiana, each part of this new nation created its own architectural landscape as its people adapted their Old World traditions to New World climate and terrain.

New England, the Middle States, the South, and the West, travelers wrote, each had a distinctive style of building and living. Over many changes and many years, that powerful distinctiveness began to fade, and by our century, there's much sameness.

But fortunately for us all, that difference and distinctiveness was still discernible when the Historic American Buildings Survey (HABS) architects, draftsmen, and photographers went on the hunt for America's early buildings.

NEW ENGLAND

The Stoughtons, a New England
farm family, pose in front of their
small Cape-style house, which is
set on the north branch of the Black
River near Perkinsville, in southern Vermont's Windsor County.

A PECULIAR PLACE, A PECULIAR RACE

New England was a peculiar place. New Englanders insisted on it.

The people of New England had a well-deserved reputation as a *race* of hard workers and shrewd bargainers. They were almost insufferably proud of their schools, their meetinghouses, their "decent morals and good order," and their descent from the Pilgrims and the Puritans. They prided themselves on their Englishness.

A lot of them also enjoyed pointing out what was wrong with the rest of America: New York City was cosmopolitan and irreligious. The New York Dutch and the Pennsylvania Germans were hardworking farmers—but unfortunately for them, they weren't English. Quakers were well behaved but had mistaken religious beliefs. Southerners were lazy because slaves did all the work. Westerners were poorly educated and often violent.

These opinions did not endear them to their fellow Americans. "Yankees" were respected but not widely loved. "The New Englanders are not an amiable people," wrote the Scotsman Thomas Hamilton in 1834, but "it must still be admitted they are a singular and original people." New Englanders wrote most of the nation's

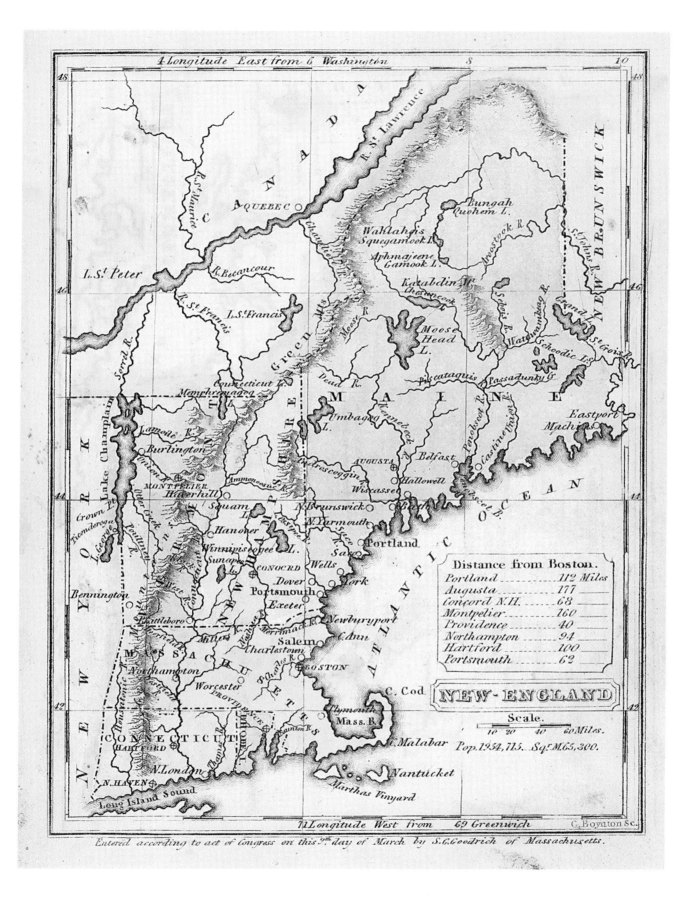

Distance from Boston.

Portland	112 Miles
Augusta	177
Concord N.H.	68
Montpelier	160
Providence	40
Northampton	94
Hartford	100
Portsmouth	62

NEW-ENGLAND

Scale.
10 20 40 60 Miles.

Pop. 1954,715. Sq.r M.65,300.

4 Longitude East from 6 Washington   8   10

71 Longitude West from   69 Greenwich   G. Boynton Sc.

Entered according to act of Congress on this 9th day of March by S.C. Goodrich of Massachusetts.

schoolbooks and shaped the writing of most American history through the 1800s. In works such as Samuel G. Goodrich's *Pictorial Geography of the World*, they penned and published authoritative descriptions of the new nation and its regions—descriptions that were well informed but with a New England slant.

A LAND OF FARMS AND STREAMS

In physical terms, the region was the smallest of the country's four. It was colder than the rest. Summers on the New England farm had lovely, transparently blue days. The fall brought the warmth and haze of Indian summer. But the New England spring was cold, foggy, muddy, and unpredictable. And winter went on forever.

It was a land of weathered mountains and rounded hills, thousands of streams, a few rich river valleys, sandy coastal plains, thin soil, and rocky shores. Its greatest natural resource was moving water. And water ran everywhere. "There is scarcely a farm without a brook, mill-stream, or river," Goodrich wrote. What it lacked in good farmland it made up for with the streams that provided water power for mills and factories, which helped New England lead the country into the Industrial Revolution.

New Englanders worked hard and viewed their progress quite literally. From the time of their first settlements in the 1620s and '30s, they steadily cleared away the old forests to build their farms. By 1840, most of the woods in Massachusetts, Rhode Island, and Connecticut had been conquered and all that was left of the towering ancient forests were thousands of farm firewood lots.

Southern New England had become a place mostly of open vistas of pasture and meadow, where families on scattered farms could see the lights of their neighbors at night. Except for the thinly settled northern parts of Maine and New Hampshire, "the whole surface of New England is checkered with cultivation," reported *The Universal Traveler* in 1836. It was a region of family farms and family labor, a patchwork of small fields and tight fences. A farmer plowed not with a horse but with an ox, which was surer footed on those sloping, stony fields. And when the ox could no longer pull, it became meat.

Thousands of farms speckled the countryside, from a few large, elegant estates practicing "scientific agriculture" to tumbledown farms whose barns and fields were a desolation. But most travelers agreed that there was something profoundly compelling about them as visible expressions of New England's way of life.

A low stone wall separates the connected buildings of the Benjamin Abbot farmhouse in Essex County, Massachusetts, from the road. The center-chimney house was built in 1685, a kitchen addition and open shed connecting the house to barn came later.

199

Built in 1799, the
Strafford Meeting-
house in Strafford,
Vermont, was used
in turn for the
services of each of
the town's Protestant
denominations.
In the 1830s it was
acquired by the town
and used solely for
town meetings
and community
functions.

(top) *One of New England's earliest houses is the Fairbanks House in Dedham, Massachusetts, built in 1636. Although most of the original casement windows have been replaced with double-hung windows, they still show the original asymmetrical window placement.*

(right) *A loom and spinning wheel are set up in an upstairs chamber of the Fairbanks House. Edward Parry described how the noise of the loom penetrated through the house.*

The great novelist Charles Dickens cast an approving eye on both land and people. Writing in his *American Notes* of 1841, he observed of New England communities that they were "as favorable specimens of rural America as their people are of rural Americans." Although Dickens did not find the ancient, carefully tended lawns of England, he saw "delicate slopes of land, gently-swelling hills, wooded valleys, and slender streams." New Englanders thought of themselves as a people with a long history in America. Dickens saw "an aspect of newness on every object."

CHILDREN OF THE PURITANS

Visitors to New England in the early 19th century usually wrote favorably of its orderly communities, well-tended farms, and the comparative equality of its people. "Wealth is more equally distributed in the New England States, than perhaps in any other country of the world," Hamilton wrote. Charles Daubney agreed that the great number of New England houses that were "suited to persons of moderate means" showed that there was less poverty and wider prosperity than anywhere he had been. Yet they also saw a good deal of self-righteousness and self-congratulation.

New Englanders needn't be so smug about their ancestors, Hamilton wrote. They should remember that the Pilgrim fathers were "full of spiritual pride, needy, bigoted, superstitious . . . fleeing from persecution in the Old World, and yet bringing it to the New." Before 1840, most of New England's people were the direct descendants of a relatively small group of English men and women, the 20,000 or so who between 1620 and 1645 crossed the Atlantic to settle in Plymouth and Massachusetts Bay, in what New Englanders came to call "the Great Migration."

After that, immigration was just a trickle for almost 200 years. This common ancestry and small size made New England the most homogeneous part of America, so that differences between north and south, east and west, village and country, town and city were more about geography than cultural identity.

The region was a landscape of small- and medium-size farms, stone walls, and distinctive wooden houses: the lean-to or saltbox, what's now called the Cape (for Cape Cod-style house), and the central-chimney house. New Englanders gathered in town meetings to govern their communities by direct vote, as virtually no one else in the country did. They built schools for their children and highly valued reading and writing. They kept the Sabbath more strictly. Because they kept careful accounts

(top) This would have been considered the "best room" in this 17th-century house, with the best chairs and best objects on display. Before houses were built with entryways, or foyers, the main entry door would have opened directly into one of the living spaces in the house.

(bottom) Wide, varied-width floorboards were common well in to the 1800s, before building began to demand lumber in consistent dimensions. The raised-panel walls in this room are signs of wealth. More ordinary houses would have had plastered or rough board walls..

Built around 1770, the "Old Joe Herrick" House in Franklin County, Massachusetts, is a sizable story-and-a-half, central-chimney house. A woodshed and workspace are in the ell out back.

and so many of them were used to scratching a living from stony soil, they gained a reputation as thrifty, even stingy—less generous than other Americans, who saw them as calculating, judgmental, and intent on business.

THE "CAPITAL" OF NEW ENGLAND

Many European travelers began their tours of America by landing in Boston, the city that New Englanders generally recognized as the center of their economy and culture. New England had smaller coastal cities, from Portland in Maine to Providence in Rhode Island, but Boston ideas, Boston manners, and Boston money dominated.

Boston was energetic and orderly. The people had "a solemnity of demeanour, not observable in their more southern neighbours," Hamilton wrote. In Boston "a shopkeeper weighs coffee or measures tape with the air of a philosopher . . . and as you walk off with your parcel in your pocket, examines you from top to toe, in order to gain some probable conclusion as to your habits or profession."

New Englanders and European visitors seemed to agree that the city, set atop its three hills, made a beautiful sight from a distance, whether riding in from the country or sailing into Boston Harbor (in those days, such topographical features could still easily be seen in a cityscape). However, once inside Boston, they again agreed (in the words of the *Pictorial Geography*) that the city had been "built, almost from the beginning, without any regard to plan, beauty or future convenience," and that its streets had been "left to fashion themselves into a tortuous intricacy."

Every visitor on record (and there are quite a few), though, made a favorable exception for the city's great open Common, which the *Geography* described "originally a cow pasture for the housekeepers of the town, but now a public park and promenade."

In 1830 the city boasted 30 banks, scores of large mercantile firms, hundreds of retail stores, and "manufactories of glass, iron, cordage, leather, chemical preparations, hats, clothing, furniture, machinery, musical instruments and . . . printing." Still, in these early years of the new republic, Boston was a city of narrow compass. The great majority of its inhabitants walked to and from their places of business.

Its streets were crowded with pedestrians but also with private coaches, hand carts, and horse-drawn freight wagons noisily delivering everything from firewood to furniture. Driving through the older parts of

This house was one of Boston's most impressive mansions when it was built in 1804. Taken in 1885, this view shows the four-story house of some 20 rooms before it was drastically changed for commercial use in downtown Boston.

HABS no. MA-167-11

This house in Boston's North End was already nearly 100 years old when Paul Revere bought it in 1770. Revere sold the house in 1800. Until 1902, when one of his descendants bought it, the house served as a rooming house and tenement.

Twenty-five years later, John Palmer passed the same way and found that the "old frame houses" had begun to disappear. Most of the buildings, he wrote in his *Journal of Travels in the United States,* "are of brick or stone, three, four or five stories high," and many of the brick houses were "painted white or stone colour." He saw the widow's walks as well but merely described them as balconies. He apparently did not see laundry hanging out to dry.

Boston, like other American cities, had a great variety of houses: tiny houses shared by several families; laborers' dwellings; the "middling" houses of craftsmen and shopkeepers; the homes of substantial merchants and lawyers; the great houses of the wealthy. (The Historic American Buildings Survey

(above) The Marshall-Hancock House, a substantial brick merchant's home, was built about 1750 to 1760. Although it was extensively remodeled as a commercial building, evidence of its use as a residence remained—at least when the HABS photographer took this shot in 1934.

(right) These elevation drawings of the Marshall-Hancock House show its façade as it might have looked in the early 1800s when it was still used as a residence.

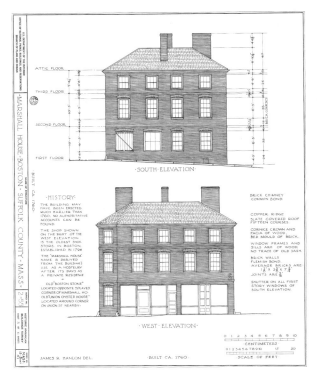

Dating to 1666, this starkly severe house in Burlington, Massachusetts, is a good example of a sizable early center-chimney house. Its original windows would have been casement types with diamond-shape leaded panes.

worthy models for our imitation," but few New Englanders outside the cities agreed. They built their religious buildings in wood, just like they built their houses in wood.

Charles Dickens added his usual touch of imagination to describing the landscape. Passing through the Massachusetts town of Worcester, he thought that "all the buildings looked as if they had been built and painted that morning, and could be taken down on Monday with very little trouble." New England houses seemed "slightly built wooden houses" with "cardboard colonnades," and their angular wooden frames had "razor-like edges" that "seemed to cut the very wind as it whistled against them." Thomas Hamilton had this same perception of newness but intensely disliked it. He remarked on "the utter flimsiness of the houses . . . . They are evidently not calculated to last above fifteen or twenty years . . . ."

George Washington may have been less visionary than Thomas Jefferson and less inventive than Benjamin Franklin, but he was another close observer and he knew his houses. While taking a goodwill tour of New England after his election to the presidency in 1789, he noticed "great similitude in their houses," which were very different from the ones he knew in Virginia. Their "general fashion," he said, was "a chimney, always of stone or brick . . . in the middle, with a staircase fronting." Elsewhere in America, chimneys were usually on or near end walls. Washington was describing New England's most distinctive house form, the central-chimney house. In all its variations it has been part of New England's built landscape for nearly 400 years.

The central-chimney house developed in two ways. It was an architectural response to New England's interminable winters to build the house around its source of heat, a square and solid chimney stack. And for most observers, this is the obvious explanation. But this house form was also an inheritance from across the Atlantic. The great majority of New England's settlers came from the southeastern region of England, Kent, and East Anglia, where this style of building had long been practiced. New England houses echoed the old-world architecture of England, which can still be seen in a few ancient English houses today.

HOUSES OF COLOR

An enduring image of New England is the white wooden house with a center chimney. But before 1800, that house would have stood out as the exception. The majority of houses—surprising to modern sensibilities—were not painted at all. Samuel Goodrich described the houses of

This painting from around 1850 shows a modest farmhouse with the "improved" landscaping and paint that had come into fashion after 1800. It has a fenced-in yard, decorative trees, and is white with green shutters—the classic look of rural New England. Courtesy Old Sturbridge Village.

The rear view of the 1653 Scotch House in Saugus, Massachusetts, shows the distinctive pilastered chimney and the unique roof form that gave the type its name, which is mostly known today as saltbox but sometimes as lean-to breakback style. When this photo was shot in 1940, the house had no paint, which would have been the normal "brown" color of most houses in the 1700s.

Elegant and imposing, this central hallway Federal house in Goshen, Connecticut, clearly displays the wealth and status of its owner. It boasts arched Palladian-style windows set into the center of the front façade of the house as well as into each gable end.

ordinary Connecticut farmers as being "the dun complexion assumed by unpainted wood, exposed to the weather."

This weathered, unpainted look was what New Englanders called "brown." The issue was cost; paint was expensive in the 1700s, and the blue, red, or yellow houses of the most prosperous families stood out sharply—and purposefully—from the dull, unpainted houses of their ordinary neighbors. Even in the seaport city of Salem, where every house could have used paint's protection from the salt spray, only the houses of the wealthy were painted. Henry Brooks recalled that in the 1780s the "houses of the common people were of the natural wood, generally pine or spruce, without paint or stain." And Salem's oldest houses, those built in the 1600s, had become "black with age."

Paint became much cheaper in the early 1800s, which is when white paint became fashionable. Eventually, its use spread down the economic scale. Most houses in large towns and in the fast-growing villages along the main roads came to be painted white, the color that ever since has defined the look of the New England landscape. By 1837, even the ancient, time-weathered appearance of Salem had been transformed, much to the disappointment of visiting Oxford professor Charles Daubney. He had been curious "to see a town, which in former days was so famous for witchcraft," but found "nothing either somber or picturesque." From the oldest to the newest, all houses had been painted yellow or white.

Paint came more slowly to poorer farmhouses and more isolated communities. Many houses remained "brown" into the 1840s. But these were the places that few travelers ever saw, accounting for the general belief that New England houses were always painted.

HOUSES OF PROSPERITY

A much more imposing version of the center-chimney house was a full two stories high (as opposed to a story and a half) and two rooms deep, downstairs and up. The ones George Washington described had "two flush stories with a very good show of sash and glass windows. The size generally is from 30 to 50 feet in length and from 20 to 30 feet in width." These houses provided significantly more living space than the old salt-box or lean-to-style houses, which at the same time were disappearing. And their size and imposing profile (at least to New England eyes) clearly suggested greater wealth and higher status.

The biggest of these center-chimney houses were frequently distinguished for the massiveness of their fireplaces and brickwork. Herman Melville, America's greatest novelist, had a deep and abiding affection for one of these old houses—and its chimney. He spent the most productive

Factory Villages

New England was where America's Industrial Revolution started in the 1790s. But it didn't begin with clanking steam engines and grimy factories. The first textile mills were built along streams in the countryside and powered by water. They were developed by ambitious New England capitalists, working at first with British "mechanics" who had smuggled their technical knowledge overseas.

Small villages, built by the mill owners, clustered around the new factories and their waterwheels. The New England families that came there to work (mostly women and children worked in the mills) became America's first industrial workers, living in company-built tenements that housed several families. Larger factory centers emerged in the early 1820s, as ways were found to tame the great rivers that flowed through New England.

Heavy investment—as the *Pictorial Geography* noted, "Much of the wealth of the capitalists of Boston is invested in the manufacturing establishments"—created the fast-growing industrial cities of Lowell, Massachusetts, and Manchester, New Hampshire.

These mills didn't hire whole families. Instead, they employed young women from the farms of New Hampshire and Vermont. These "factory girls" left their rural households to work under the discipline of factory bells and mill overseers. When not at work, they lived under the eyes of matrons in corporation-owned boardinghouses.

Top: *Boardinghouses like this one housed thousands of Lowell "mill girls" in the 1830s.* Bottom left and center left: *Before they were destroyed in a disastrous fire in 1975, the Crown and Eagle Mills in North Uxbridge, Massachusetts, built 1825–29, were one of the best-preserved early mill complexes in New England.* Bottom right and Center right: *Still standing is the Boot Mill, one of the great factory buildings that so impressed visitors to Lowell, Massachusetts after it was built in 1835. All three were surmounted by bell towers that summoned workers from their homes every morning but Sunday.*

MASS-437(a)   MASS., 3·ATBO, 3·1   HABS

Built in 1790, this impressive center-chimney colonial reflects the wealth and position of its owner and builder, Joel Robinson, who was a successful farmer and housewright who also fought in the Revolutionary War.

13 years of his writing life in a circa 1794 farmhouse in Pittsfield, Massachusetts. Initially attracted by its striking views and closeness to his friend, Nathaniel Hawthorne, he came to love the house itself. The house had eight rooms, built around a massive central chimney. To Melville, the great chimney became a personal presence, almost a companion.

He wrote his masterpiece, *Moby Dick*, in that house but also marked his stay there with a story, "I and My Chimney," in which the central chimney becomes the central character. "My chimney is the one great domineering object" that has "the center of the house" to itself, leaving "the odd holes and corners to the family," Melville's narrator says. "The walls of my house are entirely free from fire-places . . . and my family and guests . . . all sleep round one warm chimney.

"At its base in the cellar," he went on, "it is precisely twelve feet square; and hence covers precisely one hundred and forty-four superficial feet. What an appropriation of terra firma for a chimney, and what a huge load for this earth!" Melville exaggerated only a bit; the chimney of his Pittsfield house actually measured an impressive 11 feet by 11 feet at its base.

THE TINY HOUSE

Although the big and impressive central-chimney houses are what loom largest in the popular vision of New England architecture, below the threshold of visibility for most travelers in early New England were the thousands of tiny, cramped houses that usually sat out of sight, well off the main roads.

"We have but one room to eat and sit in," wrote Lieutenant Thomas Hughes in 1777 about the house where he was interned as a British prisoner of war in Pepperell, Massachusetts. The room was "in common with all the family, master, mistress and servant and what to call it, I know not, as it serves for parlour, kitchen and workroom." The parents slept in the house's other room, a tiny adjoining bedroom. Everyone else slept in "what is commonly called the garret." Hughes wrote in his journal, "At night a large fire is made on the hearth and the kitchen (or whatever it is) receives the whole family. Mother Brown and me round the fire she knitting and asking us silly questions . . . two or three women spinning with large noisy wheels and in the middle of the room sits Father and one or two apprentice boys shelling Indian corn."

Although they were gradually declining in number, such tiny houses persisted well into the 1800s. Around 1810, the farmer and livestock drover Asa Sheldon spent the night in one of these two-room New England houses, an experience that stuck in his memory. He recalled the "two small glass windows in front and a board one at the rear" and the fact that its thin wooden sheathing had never been covered by clapboards. What made it "a unique habitation," however, was the "pine post near the fireplace" that had been added to prop up the sagging floor of the garret above. "So much had been hewed off for kindlings," he wrote, that at the bottom it had been almost whittled down to a sliver.

As late as 1835 New Englanders occasionally encountered living conditions that they thought had been left far in the past. The young bookbinder Homer Merriam spent nearly four months in the house of Rhoda Rhodes, an elderly healing woman, part Yankee and part Mahican Indian. He had suffered from an unknown illness for a couple of years and, dissatisfied with doctors, had come to try out the old lady's herbal cures. She too, "lived in a house of two rooms and an attic," Merriam recalled. "One room was used for a storeroom only, and the other was

(top) An appropriately impressive entry with turned columns and a cove ceiling let passersby know that this house in North Stonington, Connecticut, belongs to a family with means and position. The wealth that built this house probably came from fishing, whaling, or the overseas trade.

(bottom) Built in the late 1600s or early 1700s in Newington, New Hampshire, the Newington Parsonage is a substantial two-story center-chimney house that would have reflected a fairly high degree of prosperity.

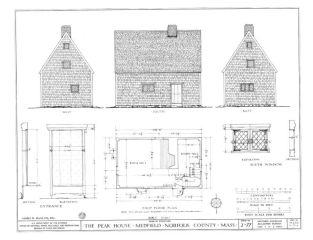

(above) The Samuel Moore House in Hartford, Connecticut, was built in about 1700 and shows the clear, strong lines of a New England lean-to or breakback house, more commonly known today as a saltbox. Most were built with a standard gable roof, but as the family grew in size and prosperity, the first-floor shed addition on the back would be added to give the roof its unique slope.

(below and facing page) Many New England houses were as small or smaller than the Peak House in Medfield, Massachusetts. Thanks perhaps to its stark appearance and steep gable roof, it survived. The size of its first floor is less than 400 sq. ft., much of that dominated by the huge chimney.

the kitchen, parlor and the old lady's bedroom. Visitors, of which there were sometimes several, sleeping in the attic, which was divided into bedrooms, as occasion might require, by hanging up blankets or sheets for partitions."

Merriam was struck by the house's window arrangements and dark interior. Downstairs were three small windows, one completely boarded up and another partially blocked. Upstairs, the garret had one glassless window that could be shut using a couple of boards. "When I rose in the morning, I removed one of the boards to let in the light to see to dress by," he wrote. Another feature of the house was equally striking. When he woke up, he "could look down through the floor of the attic to see when breakfast was ready."

The house's dark interior may have been explained by Native American cultural preference for a more intimate domestic space—or it may simply have reflected Rhoda's unwillingness to replace window glass. Dark and dilapidated as the house was, Homer's stay there was successful. He "improved very decidedly in health" and left there feeling much better.

LEAN-TOS AND BREAKBACKS

Probably the most classic and memorable of New England central-chimney houses had a two-story front and a long roofline sloping down to one story in the rear. It went by several names. "Saltbox" is the most familiar term, reflecting the look of a once familiar container. New Englanders were more likely to call it a "breakback," as they would say in Connecticut, or a "lean-to," which folks in Massachusetts favored. The lean-to form took a four-room house plan—two rooms below, two above—and enlarged it to include a sizable kitchen.

As an old man, Charles Hyde described the lean-to house where he grew up in the first decade of the 1800s. It was "built with its length along the line of the street . . . . In the front were two rooms, between which was the door opening onto a narrow passage. From the passage-way doors led to each front room, and a staircase turning twice at right angles with landings in the corners, led to the chambers above. The kitchen . . . occupied most of the rear half. A small bedroom was cut off from the end. A side door, the pantry, and cellarway occupied the other end."

The saltbox was not a poor man's house but a sign of moderate prosperity. (The less well-off lived in one-story houses or in "two over two" structures that didn't have the extended kitchen.) For much of the 1700s, lean-tos, with their two-story façades, were the characteristic houses of comfortable (although not wealthy) farm families. But like today, the old gradually yielded to larger houses.

Traveling across New England in the 1930s, Historic American Buildings Survey crews photographed a number of old houses in the process of destruction and decay. Some revealed otherwise hidden details of construction. Others simply recorded the progress of dissolution. A few told stories.

The Elam House, built in 1784 in Middleton, Rhode Island, tells a story of partial preservation. Built as a sizable Georgian central-hallway house, it was extensively rebuilt in 1803 in the grand Federal style by its new owner, just arrived from England. Yet by 1937 its old elegance had wasted away into an abandoned wreck. No trace of it exists today, with one exception: Its elegantly carved front doorway was saved and added to the collections of the Metropolitan Museum of Art in New York.

George Jacobs's house in Danvers, Massachusetts, told a very different story. Built in the mid 1600s, it was a center-chimney farmhouse with an asymmetrical plan characteristic of the 1600s—a large "hall" and smaller "parlor" downstairs with three small upstairs bedchambers. (Additions and outbuildings came later in the 18th century.) In 1692, it was the scene of terrible events, part of New England's last spasm of witch belief and persecution. Accused by his own granddaughter, Margaret, George Jacobs was taken from this house, tried for witchcraft, convicted, and hung on Gallows Hill in Salem. "I am falsely accused," he maintained. His family's life was left in ruins for at least a generation, but the house survived into the 1920s. When last photographed in 1935, this ancient house with its tragic history had become a ruin itself.

A few miles from the Jacobs House was another dwelling linked to the witchcraft terror. For three years in the 1680s it had been the home of the Rev. George Burroughs, then serving as minister of what was then called Salem Village. Accused along with Jacobs, he was targeted as the "Black Minister," the leader of the witches' coven in Salem. Burroughs too was arrested, brought to trial, and hung on Gallows Hill that same year.

Burroughs's old house was known as the Putnam House, and probably dating to the 1650s, that house had long disappeared by the time HABS surveyors came to Danvers in 1935. Instead, they documented the new house that succeeded it: William Landers had bought the ancient house in 1841 and then demolished the relic of a dark past. On the site he built anew in his time's most modern style, a tranquil Grecian with symmetrical Corinthian columns, double doors, and side porches, and set it in a landscape of shade trees, garden paths, and flower beds. Later it would become a serene setting for the last years of the poet and essayist John Greenleaf Whittier. By 1940 the new house had become a historical artifact.

Ruins

Top left: *The Nathaniel Baker House, a large center-chimney house in Connecticut's Middlesex County, was built in 1690 and was a collapsing ruin when it was photographed by a HABS photographer in 1937.* **Top right:** *George Jacobs, who built this house in 1658 in Danvers, Massachusetts, was later tried as a witch and hung. The house fell to ruins by 1938, when this photograph was taken.* **Bottom left:** *This view shows the Pidge Tavern in Pawtucket, Rhode Island, as a virtual ruin. It was begun in 1700, enlarged in 1767, turned into a tavern in 1783, and after years of neglect, demolished in the late 1930s.* **Bottom right:** *The 1697 Job Greene House in Warwick, Rhode Island, was in ruins by the time a HABS photographer shot this photograph in 1937. Although parts of the house were moved to the Rhode Island School of Design, the remainder of the house was demolished.*

CONN-33

CONN., 5-MAD., 3-1   HABS

The David Field House in Madison, Connecticut, is a lean-to house built around 1720. A descendent of the builder was Cyrus West Field, who laid the Atlantic cable that connected North America to Europe via telegraph in 1866.

Lean-to houses dwindled, not because they were no longer practical but because they were no longer fashionable. The town historian of Berlin, Massachusetts, estimated that in 1830 "one-third, perhaps" of the town's houses "were of the long back roofs of one story and two stories front." But two generations later, they had disappeared completely. "Our last," he wrote, "went down in smoke, 1886."

A NEW SIGN OF WEALTH

Toward the middle of the 1700s, England sent a new kind of architecture to New England and to the rest of America. Later called the Georgian style after the succession of English kings of that name, the style favored symmetry, formality, and order.

Builders of the earliest New England houses put windows and doors wherever they were needed. In some cases one window would be positioned above another, while a third, fourth, and more were inserted seemingly at random, almost design after-thoughts. Symmetry was either never considered or at least never considered to be that important.

But the classic Georgian house had a completely symmetrical façade of doors and windows, with identical chimney stacks at both ends, two (or three) stories, each one two rooms wide and two rooms deep. Its most dramatic feature was a central passage or hallway that ran all the way through the house. All doors opened on to the hallway, and a highly visible (and highly desirable from a status point of view) staircase ascended to the next floor. This plan provided greater privacy, separating family and visitors and made entering the house a formal, rather than an intimate and neighborly, experience.

New England's wealthiest were the first to build in this new way, after learning about it from relatives or business contacts in England or from books. In no time at all, the central-hallway house became a fashion statement; its different look on the landscape proclaimed its owners' wealth and their position of leadership in their communities.

These houses were dramatically different in another way. Doors, windows, rooflines, and corners were decorated with elaborate designs taken from the architecture of the classical world. Doorways were capped by pediments and flanked by pilasters. Rooflines and windows were embellished with cornices and dentils.

Foreign travelers were not always impressed. The Scotsman Thomas Hamilton wrote in 1832 of ". . . the glaring effect arising from the too profuse application of the paint-brush," noting that the "extreme fragility" of their wood construction "renders more glaring the absurdity of that profusion of gewgaw decoration in which the richer inhabitants delight to indulge." Still, Americans loved them.

All of these classical details together told this story: that the men who owned these houses were gentlemen who had had a traditional education in Greek and Latin and were intimately familiar with the ancient world. This was actually true only for a few; not many New England merchants, lawyers, and landowners were really classical scholars. Still, pilasters and pediments served for a long time as a powerful badge of status.

During the 1700s and up through 1820 or so, the central-hallway house was widely taken up by New England's prosperous families. Some built smaller versions, "single-pile" houses that were only one room deep. Their basic form didn't change, but details and proportions did, as architecture moved from the Georgian style to what historians now call the Federal style in the 1790s.

The original structure was built in the mid-1700s as a seaman's hide-away for Captain Richard Charleton of Norwichtown, Connecticut. His son added on to it, creating the modest lean-to roofline. Although most saltbox-style houses are larger two-story center-chimney houses, the style of this house is based on the traditional Cape Cod design.

These houses have been called "Cape houses" or "Capes" ever since, but the name is a bit misleading. True, they were almost universal along the sandy roads of the Cape, but more important, the houses he described would have been found just about all over New England, as they are today.

Dwight didn't notice these houses elsewhere in his travels because his eye was distracted. Although he grudgingly noted that "a great proportion" of the houses on Cape Cod were " in good repair," it was clear that he didn't really like them. They were low on the landscape and too small. Smaller structures, he thought, could not be elegant or even comfortable.

(above) One of New England's great Georgian houses was built by merchant prince Jeremiah Lee a few years before the American Revolution. In 1804 it became the building for the first bank in Marblehead, Massachusetts, and remained a bank headquarters for more than a hundred years until it was acquired and restored by the local historical society.

(right) With its luxurious diamond-pattern brickwork and enclosed pediment gables, the Governor Martin Chittenden House in Chittenden County, Vermont, is a graphic example of the Federal style.

Gaols

If you had been arrested for a crime, fallen into debt, or, sometimes, become mentally ill, you would have been sent to one of New England's county jails, or "gaols," as the traditional spelling went. Like local taverns, gaols were built like large houses and acted as an extended household—although a specialized and unpleasant one.

The sheriff, or gaoler, responsible for the prisoners lived there with his family. His wife, daughters, or domestic helpers cooked for the prisoners and served them their meals, and the movement of prisoners in and out was part of the family's everyday life.

The jail of York County in Maine, which functioned from the late 1600s until 1860, was abundantly documented by the HABS survey, which lets us see how these institutions worked.

The jail was in part a two-story framed house with a parlor, sitting room, and bedchambers. It was also a stone dungeon with 2-ft.-thick walls and a completely exposed indoor privy. The first-floor dungeon cells had no outside windows at all, although prisoners could look out into a small gallery. The upper cells, for lesser offenders, had thinner walls and a few tiny barred windows. Imprisoned debtors had more windows and a larger cell.

Top: *Violently breaking the law wasn't the only infraction that might land a New Englander in prison. The cells in this barnlike structure were used to confine mentally ill inmates of the Barnstable County poor farm in Massachusetts.* Left: *The Old York Gaol in York, Maine, looks much like a gambrel-roof house. It would have been a home for the warden and his family, although the stone dungeon walls were 2 ft. thick.* Center: *Privacy wasn't an issue for inmates in the Old York Gaol, which dates back to the 17th century. A prisoner using this privy would have been completely exposed.* Right: *The floor plan of the Old York Gaol illustrates an arresting contrast: the family's parlor and the prisoners dungeon cell.*

Hawthorne and the New England House

Nathaniel Hawthorne was born July 4, 1804, in an older but comfortable gambrel-roofed central-chimney house. Salem, Massachusetts, was then a busy seaport, one of New England's great centers of shipping and trade. When his ship captain father died at sea in 1808, he and his suddenly impoverished mother went to live with her parents. This house, which the writer barely remembered, has been preserved and restored as a historical landmark.

Hawthorne became a restless walker of Salem's streets who came to know the town's old houses very well. Of one of these he wrote, "Halfway down a by-street of one of our New England towns stands a rusty wooden house, with seven acutely pointed gables, facing toward various points of the compass."

He had never lived in that "rusty wooden house," built in 1668, but he was struck by the unusual multiple peaks and gables, the result of numerous additions and changes, and its secret staircase. The house became the model for the brooding, secretive, death-haunted structure at the center of his *The House of the Seven Gables*. The house is both the novel's setting and a character in its own right,

a symbol for the shaping, even distorting, power the past has over the present.

Hawthorne left Salem in 1842 for rural Concord. There he found another house that would engage his imagination. "Between the two tall gate-posts of rough-hewn stone," he wrote, "we beheld the gray front of the old parsonage," owned since 1776 by Concord's Congregational minister. "It was awful to reflect how many sermons must have been written there," Hawthorne thought.

The "old manse" was a spacious central-hallway house with a dozen rooms and a gambrel roof. But the house had aged greatly. Its unpainted clapboards had weathered to a dull gray-brown, contrasting with the newer and better-maintained "white houses" of Concord village.

Hawthorne found the house a good place to write, and he enjoyed using the old minister's study. The house, he said, had ghosts enough to stimulate his imagination. While there he wrote his first significant work of fiction, a book of stories that he called *Mosses from an Old Manse*, published in 1846.

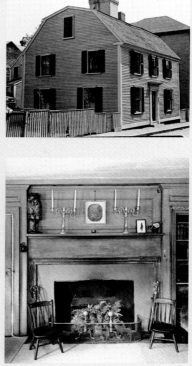

Top: *This gambrel-roofed central-chimney house in Salem, Massachusetts, is preserved as Nathaniel Hawthorne's birthplace. When his sea captain father died on a voyage, the four-year-old Hawthorne and his mother moved into his mother's parents' house nearby.* **Facing page:** *Hawthorne's solitary walks through Salem to avoid the cramped conditions he endured while living with relatives led him to appreciate this ancient house, which belonged to some cousins. The house later became the model for one of Hawthorne's great novels,* The House of Seven Gables. **Left:** *In 1842, Hawthorne and his wife moved into the Old Manse House, formerly owned by a Congregational minister. It was here that he wrote his first notable work of fiction,* Mosses from an Old Manse. *Hawthorne found the old minister's study,* **Above,** *to be an encouraging space for his writing.*

Dwight was a regional patriot, eager to defend his part of the country and trumpet its virtues, but he dismissed Capes as "small and mean." However, the French revolutionary Brissot de Warville admired the small houses of New England. In 1788 he described the country houses occupied by small farmers and craftsmen, some a story and a half with finished bed-chambers and others with "but one story and a garret." He was probably a bit overoptimistic (if we remember Edward Parry's encounter with the Parker family in Sturbridge) when he claimed that "neatness embellishes them all." Still, he thought, they were pretty decent places to live. There was coffee and tea on their tables, sometimes wallpaper on their walls, and their daughters could dress respectably.

(above) Walking into the Ma'am Lee cottage, a visitor would have had to go straight upstairs or walk directly into one of the house's two main rooms. Behind the winder stairway is a huge central chimney that took up a substantial portion of the first-floor space.

(right) A national favorite today, the Cape Cod-style house is a classic New England form. This is an example of a double Cape, which means it has two "bents" or structural bays on each side of the chimney and four windows on the long elevation. Single Capes would have had only two bays and two windows, and a three-quarters Cape would have had three bays and three windows on the long side.

STEVEN WALKLEY BUILDS A HOUSE

The Walkleys of Southington, Connecticut, were an ordinary family living in one of these houses. Thanks to their reminiscences and a surviving account book (the ledger people used to keep track of what they borrowed from and exchanged with their neighbors), we know quite a bit about how their house was built and what their life was like. (The HABS survey team missed the Walkley House but documented many similar ones.) "I gladly look back to the house, where nine of us children were born," Mary Angeline Walkley Beach wrote in 1877. It was "a story and a half . . . with a large chimney in the center around which there were three fire places and several cupboards and closets." It fronted the road to the west, and like many unpretentious houses in the New England countryside, "it had never been painted" while she was growing up.

Her father, Steven Walkley, was never wealthy, Mary Angeline recalled. He owned "a small, poor farm" and surveyed land for farmers in the surrounding towns. His account

Built in about 1725, this Cape, called the Ma'am Lee cottage in Manchester, Massachusetts, has a gambrel roof that added height and headroom to the upper floor, which in most Capes would have been a half-story. The cottage was originally only one room deep, although a later shed addition off the back provided a bit more space.

The Ephraim Harding House in Massachusetts' Cape Cod town of Truro was a "three-quarters" Cape built around 1820.

book shows that in 1808, at the age of 21, he acquired a piece of land and began to build his house. He took years to complete it, working himself and hiring others episodically as the agricultural calendar, other men's schedules, and his funds permitted. His accounts show us that he did as much as he could on his own but needed to call on his nearby neighbors and on some highly skilled artisans in the community.

Over the course of six months, Steven got the basic structure put up. Using money that he had saved and exchanging for his own labor, he found men with skills in stonework who dug the cellar, laid the foundation stones, and built the fireplace and chimney. He hired a skilled housewright to hew the house's structural timbers and to mark and lay out the frame. Others supplied shingles and clapboards. Most of these men joined forces with neighboring farmers to help him raise the frame in mid-May. He then found another local carpenter who worked quickly with him to enclose the house with sheathing boards and then to nail on the clapboards to finish the outside. Three weeks after the frame was raised, he moved in.

Walkley was young and unmarried. He was willing to live in an unfinished house and work his small farm while he slowly finished the interior. Over the next year, he built a rough set of stairs up to the garret and put down upstairs flooring. Today, we call that "sweat equity."

Three years later, in 1811, Steven Walkley married Olive Newell and brought his young wife to live in the still unfinished house. The next weeks found him installing stone steps for the front door and making a picket fence for the dooryard. Improvements took time. It was not until 1816, after the first three children had been born, that the Walkleys had their downstairs rooms lathed and plastered.

The upstairs remained a rough garret until the mid-1820s, when the two bedchambers were finally finished, and Steven and Olive moved their bed upstairs. In addition to Steven and Olive's nine children, the house also made room for Steven's father and two unmarried sisters. "Such was my house," wrote Mary Angeline, "humble, unpretending."

THE NEW "END" HOUSES

By 1820, a new type of house appeared in New England, one that broke radically with tradition. Like the Georgian and Federal styles, what we now call the Greek Revival style emerged out of the classical past. But this time it directly imitated the form, as well as the details, of classical buildings—the temples of ancient Greece.

In a building contract for one of these houses in 1828, housewright Joel Upham described what was different about the new plan, which dramatically transformed the look of the house on the landscape. He called it an "end house." For centuries almost all buildings had been oriented "longways," with the main door and the façade presented to the outside and set in the long side of the house. Houses, meetinghouses, and schools all had their rooflines running parallel to the line of the road.

But the new style reoriented the house a full 90 degrees to the road, to match the alignment of Grecian buildings. Each house was a domestic version of an Athenian temple, with its dramatic pediment and graceful pillars.

The Grecian house or end house presented its gable end, and the peak of its roof, to the road. The front door was usually placed on one side of the gable end, and visitors passed through a long "side hall" to enter rooms that were located behind each other, no longer paired on either side of the doorway. Even more than the central-hallway house, the Grecian house provided for the family's privacy and the separation of living space from the entryway. Greek Revival houses became immensely popular in New England in the 1830s, but not everyone admired them.

(top) The steep, narrow stairs of this c. 1810 house in Norwichtown, Connecticut are tucked against the parlor fireplace.

(below) A local artist sketched the Jepthah Plimpton House in Brookfield, Massachusetts, in 1840. A classical Cape form, the house and its outbuildings were at the center of the family farm.

Schools

Returning after a trip west, the minister and teacher Henry Dana Ward crossed into Massachusetts and noted in his travel journal that he was "back in the land of schools."

Throughout most of New England (everywhere except Rhode Island) and driven by the Puritan concern that New England children learn to read the Bible and the catechism, the law required towns to provide schools, at public expense. As a result, New England had one of the highest rates of literacy in the world. By the 1790s, there were thousands of one-room schoolhouses scattered across the landscape. Most families lived no more than a couple of miles from one—a challenging trip in the winter but one that generations of New England children were used to.

"District schools," as they were called, were tax supported and directly controlled by the families in each country neighborhood. Funded sparingly by tax dollars, they were relatively slight structures, often built without clapboards and sited on otherwise unusable land. Still, they were symbols of New England's commitment to education, enterprise, and good order, and New Englanders were enduringly proud of them.

After 1790, something new arose across New England (and elsewhere in America): institutions (hundreds of them) called academies or seminaries, responding to the needs of aspiring young men and women seeking education beyond the common schools. A few were denominationally inspired; most were private establishments. Students came to attend for one, two, or three half-year terms, although rarely more than three years. Academic standards in these new schools varied. Some provided a fairly rigorous curriculum of languages, science, and history; most academies for young women emphasized painting, music, and ornamental needlework.

Most of them were built as large houses, although a few resembled meetinghouses. At the top of the educational pyramid, Harvard, Yale, and Brown were New England's traditional, long-established collegiate institutions. Yet they were institutions of modest scale, serving only a handful of students—mostly the children of New England's elite. College students lived in a strange mix of strict regulation and laxity. Pages of rules governed their conduct, but there were frequent student riots and traditions of bacchanalian celebration. Walking in the Massachusetts town of Cambridge in 1823, Henry Kendall noted that "at Harvard college, even the youngest students chew and smoke; boys may be seen with cigars in their mouths."

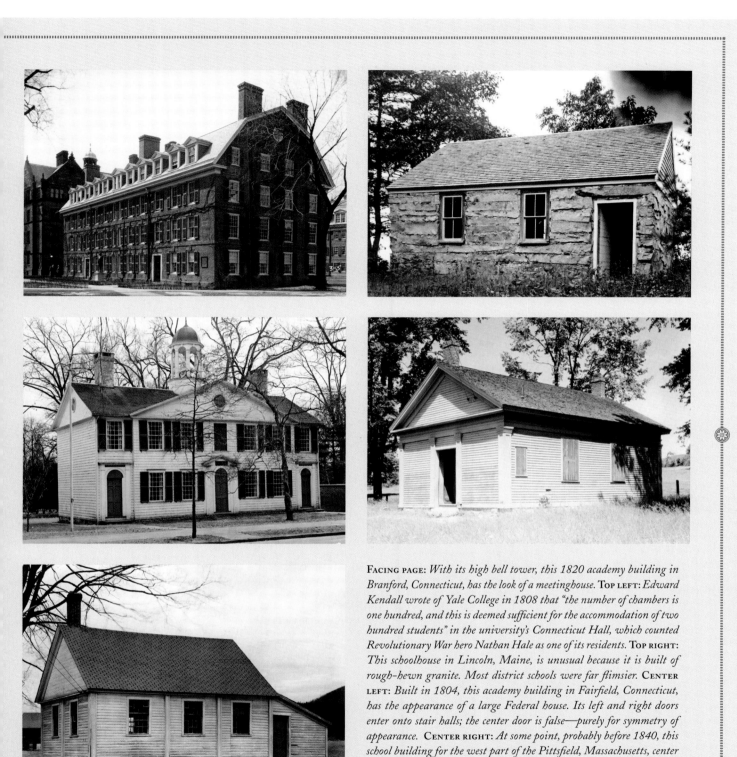

FACING PAGE: *With its high bell tower, this 1820 academy building in Branford, Connecticut, has the look of a meetinghouse.* TOP LEFT: *Edward Kendall wrote of Yale College in 1808 that "the number of chambers is one hundred, and this is deemed sufficient for the accommodation of two hundred students" in the university's Connecticut Hall, which counted Revolutionary War hero Nathan Hale as one of its residents.* TOP RIGHT: *This schoolhouse in Lincoln, Maine, is unusual because it is built of rough-hewn granite. Most district schools were far flimsier.* CENTER LEFT: *Built in 1804, this academy building in Fairfield, Connecticut, has the appearance of a large Federal house. Its left and right doors enter onto stair halls; the center door is false—purely for symmetry of appearance.* CENTER RIGHT: *At some point, probably before 1840, this school building for the west part of the Pittsfield, Massachusetts, center village was given some Greek Revival trim.* BOTTOM: *A one-room schoolhouse in South Deerfield, Massachusetts, has a side entry porch that also contains a wood shed and privies for the students.*

In 1832, Thomas Hamilton traveled through the Connecticut Valley and noticed dozens of houses in the new style. He was profoundly unimpressed with these "white framework villas" with "Corinthian or Ionic columns sadly out of proportion." They were totally "out of place when attached to a wooden building." To his eyes, these attempts to re-create Greek stonework with American lumber were "simply absurd."

Yet this doesn't seem to have been the majority verdict. Other travelers enjoyed these wooden houses as American translations of the Greek idiom. They found them "charming" and "light and airy" versions of the monumental marble originals that inspired them. After 1830, very few New England houses were built in the old way. But the triumph of the end house or side-hall house was complete, and the gable end form continued long after Greek Revival details were replaced by other fashions.

LIFE IN A COLD PLACE

The rest of America thought of New England as a cold place with a short growing season and a severe and variable climate, which of course it is. "The winters are much colder, and the summers hotter than under the same parallels in Europe," the *Geography* noted.

This last bit had been a hard lesson to learn. The first couple of generations that came to New England had expected to grow oranges and lemons. After all, Cape Cod was at the same latitude as the south of France. They waited for the cycle of harsh weather to end, but it never did. It was puzzling. Not surprisingly, they didn't know that western Europe, unlike America's Atlantic coast, is warmed by the Gulf Stream. Yet they remained to struggle with the poor soil and the difficult weather. It probably was for the best. They became a people who thrived on adversity and whose pride grew in correlation with life's difficulty.

The short growing season shaped New Englanders' lives. The months between April and October were the window of time for farmwork. An unusually cold or "backward" spring spelled trouble for the crops, as did a too-early killing frost in September. New England's most important harvest was the hay crop that fed livestock over the long winter, and farm families worked furiously in the fields every summer to bring it in.

Even the conception of children varied by the season, reflecting work and nutrition. By far the fewest conceptions were in the summer months

Josiah Hayden's house in Williamsburg, Massachusetts, shown in front and side views, displays the classic elements of the new Greek Revival style of architecture that swept the country at the beginning of the 19th century. With its gable end facing the street, this house has a classic temple form with pediment supported by two-story pillars (facing page). The wings on each side (above) had pillared portions and end pediments. The style saw its most extravagant expression in the grand plantation houses of the Deep South.

of July and August, a time when men—and many women—were exhausted from 14-hour days in the hay fields. Conceptions peaked in the late fall and early winter, when the harvest had been gathered and there was time to rest, celebrate, and get on with life.

The approach of the long winter transformed life. Living space contracted and homes were kept firmly shut. Most families huddled closely around the fireplace and, at bedtime, reluctantly took their way from the hearth's pool of heat "to bedchambers that never knew a fire, where the very sheets and blankets seemed so full of stinging cold air that they made one's fingers tingle," Harriet Beecher Stowe wrote. Throughout the house "the cider would freeze in the cellar . . . the bread in the milk room would be like blocks of ice," and pies would be stored frozen in the attic.

Ice was everywhere in pitchers and washbasins. Households that had given up the use of fully hung beds for reasons of style and cleanliness often dragged them back out to keep warm. "We wore our great coats in the house half the time," Anne Jeanne Lyman remembered.

As if counseling on a moral issue, advice books simply urged Americans to bear with it. Young people were admonished by a Boston writer that "a great deal of time is wasted, in winter, in hovering over the fire and talking of the cold." What they needed was to keep busy and display "a little resolution."

Families did not insulate their houses in the modern sense but usually banked up their foundations with leaves as winter stalked nearer. Rags and old newspapers were used to seal up cracks in walls, and worn-out hats were stuffed into broken windows. The more efficient homeowner tacked pieces of wool baize or Morocco leather as weather stripping to the bottom of their doors or sealed them with long, narrow bags filled with sand. The most forward looking way of dealing with winter, and available only to the wealthy, were windows made with double sashes, precursors to modern storm windows.

Most New Englanders grew up with memories similar to the ones Harriet's husband, Calvin Stowe, had of "quitting my warm bed in a room where the thermometer must have stood below zero, and where the snow, drifting through the loosely framed window, often lay in long wreaths on the floor." On a cold January day in 1810, the Rev. William Bentley of Salem, Massachusetts, documented wintry discomfort with scientific exactitude, using his thermometer, then a rare instrument. "In my own Chamber on Saturday," he wrote, "with a brisk fire, I found the Therm. on the southern side of the Chamber at the greatest distance from the fire at 3 P.M. 16° Far. below freezing."

Most houses in early New England would have at least one great fireplace, which was used for both cooking and heat. This wide fireplace includes an iron crane to hold pots over the fire as well as the tin oven that would be set over the hot coals.

Like a modern couple arguing over the best way to stop a baby's crying, Harriet Beecher Stowe described households where married couples "had their own opinions" about the complex art of building a fire, with the husband insisting that he "was the only reasonable fire-builder," while his wife stoutly maintained "that men never knew how to build a fire."

Other New Englanders recalled instead brutally hard work: chopping down trees, hauling logs and cutting them to length, and the repetitive labor, often several times a day, of bringing in "all of this green wood, and snowy at that" to feed the fire.

Eventually, however, the reign of what Benjamin Franklin called "the fireplaces of our fathers" was challenged. This was due in good part to an improved understanding of heat, provided by two New England-born Americans: Franklin, the Revolutionary patriot, and the exiled loyalist Benjamin Thompson (later Count Rumford). Franklin invented a stove, later much modified by others, that finally brought the heat source—and the heat—into the room where warmth radiated out rather than convecting up the chimney.

Death rates, particularly for older people, were at their highest in January and February, the bleakest months of winter. The Deacon William Leland House in Sherborn, Massachusetts, is shown here during the dead of winter.

Taverns

European travelers were surprised to find that New England tavern keepers were not the subservient and deferential hosts they were used to. In New England, tavern keepers were men of local distinction and owned sizable farms. Taverns were strictly regulated, and authorities only licensed men of "good character and reputation."

Taverns were usually no more than substantial houses. The innkeeper's family lived in part of the house and took care of travelers. Wives and daughters cooked meals and tended to bedding. The landlord himself or a son tended bar; other sons or hired men took care of travelers' horses.

Because the country was growing—and moving—so fast, the tavern business became a growth industry. New and bigger taverns were built; older taverns were modernized. Most of the taverns in this book showed signs of additions and enlargements. Some had the upstairs divided into several small chambers; others simply provided a couple of large rooms crowded with beds.

After 1800, taverns were the primary links in the network of roads and stagecoaches that tied the region together. They were also major centers for community life. Farmers gathered there to drink and talk during the winter lull. Tavern ballrooms hosted dances through the winter. Stagecoach drivers and travelers brought news from Boston and elsewhere. Itinerant artists and instructors passed through, staying a week or two to paint portraits, teach dancing or singing, sell patent medicines, or even extract teeth.

Because they temporarily housed many famous figures, taverns acquired a sort of secondhand celebrity. Pawtucket, Rhode Island's Pidge Tavern was the young Marquis de Lafayette's favorite New England lodging during the Revolution. When he returned to America as an elderly man in 1823, he insisted on staying there again. The house's hospitality clearly had some attractions.

One of the most architecturally ambitious country taverns ever built in New England was built in the 1790s by Eli Wheelock in Charlton, Massachusetts to serve the traffic on a newly built turnpike road. Later sold to Colonel Isaiah Rider, the structure measures 32 ft. deep by an extraordinary 90 ft. long. Although it functioned as a tavern for 30 years, it never really fulfilled Rider's expectations. Only a portion of the building was ever used for guests—one section had to be permanently rented out.

FACING PAGE: *Tavern signs like the two-sided one shown here—with a Napoleonic figure painted on one side and an Indian on the other—were required by law to bear the proprietor's name and in some states the year of his license.* TOP: *The Rider Tavern was a three-story, 21-room, 90-ft.-long by 32-ft.-wide tavern and inn in Charlton, Massachusetts, and a particularly large example of its kind. The tavern dates from 1797, when a distiller name Eli Wheelock built his inn on the road between Worcester and Hartford, Connecticut.* BOTTOM: *The barred enclosure in a tavern barroom prevented the valuable bottles of liquor from theft or unauthorized use. Here, in the main room of the Captain Arah Phelphs Inn in Colebrook, Connecticut, the "bar" is in the far corner above the circular partition.*

In many meetinghouses, such as the Old Indian Church in Mashpee, Massachusetts (right), young men were assigned to sit up in the gallery during services so their youthful energy wouldn't disrupt their elders during a sermon. One worshipper spent his time at worship creating this elaborate carving of a ship on the gallery's front rail (above).

Rumford demonstrated how fireplaces could be redesigned for greater fuel efficiency and better heating. Economic realities played a powerful role as well. In the longer-settled parts of New England, firewood was becoming scarcer and more expensive, and in response, fireplaces had begun to grow gradually smaller by the later 1700s. After Rumford's influential essays on fireplaces were published in 1796 and 1798, fireplaces grew smaller still, as masons and housewrights incorporated the narrower chimney throats and more sharply angled sides that Rumford recommended.

After 1800, stoves were in use to heat stores, schools, and other public buildings, but it took longer for them to appear in New England homes. Cookstoves were the first to arrive, coming into kitchens in large numbers after 1820. Improved design, manufacturing, and expanded marketing led to their acceptance in city and village households, where, it was promised, they would reduce the use of firewood by two-thirds or more. They were followed in the 1830s by fully enclosed parlor stoves designed to both decorate and warm the rest of the house.

Farm families, who didn't have to buy wood, took longer to adopt stoves than those in cities and villages, but eventually they did as well. Just about everyone welcomed greater warmth, but quite a few mourned the boxing up of the flame. For New Englanders used to a cheerful fireside, said the Barre, Massachusetts, *Gazette,* the stove was "a lonesome companion to sit by during winter evenings." After her mother's cookstove was installed, Susan Blunt recalled, she and her brothers and sisters missed the "bright and cheerful" glow of the kitchen. By the 1850s, the stove had taken over almost completely, and fireplace tools became relics.

But the glow of the fireside didn't disappear for good. Fireplaces returned to popularity with the introduction of central heating in the early 1900s—once New Englanders could have both comfort and the enjoyment of the dancing flames.

A scene from a New England winter is illustrated in this early 19th-century painting. Smoke rises from the center chimney of a lean-to house as a cart delivers a load of firewood. A large farmhouse in northern New England might burn as many as 40 cords of wood over the course of a winter.

WHERE WE PRAYED

The emblem of the New England community, rising above the town common, is the graceful meetinghouse spire. Both symbolically and practically, the meetinghouse was at the center of town life because, for most of New England's history, meetinghouses were both for worship and for conducting town affairs. After the Revolution, the religious landscape became more diverse, although still overwhelmingly Protestant.

Quakers were once banished from Massachusetts but later returned as a small but significant minority. This view of the 1703 Society of Friends Meetinghouse in North Pembroke, Massachusetts, shows the entry porch with its separate men's and women's entrances, characteristic of Quaker practice. Movable partitions inside the church maintained the separation between the sexes during worship services (top right).

(above) Part of the upstairs gallery in the Chestnut Hill Meetinghouse near Millville, Massachusetts, was marked out as the "Negro Pew"— a separate seating area for people of color. Before slavery was abolished in Massachusetts in 1783, the community's small number of household slaves sat here.

(left) This round meetinghouse in Richmond, Vermont, is an architectural oddity, but its style expressed its purpose; it was built in 1813 to house the worship of five separate, but cooperating, Protestant denominations.

A remarkable view shows the spiral stair from the first to the second floor of this Gloucester, Massachusetts, Universalist church, the first built in this country.

By the early 1800s, several different denominations were represented around the town common.

Some called their buildings a "meetinghouse," others preferred "church." Finally, as church and state separated in the early 1800s, communities began to build separate town houses or town halls for civil affairs. Many smaller towns, however, continued to use the oldest meetinghouse in town for town meetings and elections, even past the Civil War. Amid New England's sea of steepled meetinghouses and a number of Methodist and Episcopal churches, a few more exotic religious buildings could be found. There were a few early Catholic churches, serving small Irish communities; a small Lutheran church in Waldoboro, Maine, for a tiny community of German immigrants; and the remarkable Touro synagogue of Newport, Rhode Island, that served early New England's only Jewish community, congregation Jeshuat Israel.

But even in an ocean of steeples, the meetinghouse was distinguished from what other denominations called churches by their lack of images, statues, altars, and other ornamentation. They were built as severely plain structures. This lack of distraction allowed worshippers to focus solely on the unadorned word of God as it was delivered to them by the minister, whose high pulpit dominated the interiors of all meetinghouses.

The typical New England meetinghouse—long and narrow and topped with a soaring steeple above the main entry, which is set into the end of the building—wasn't always that way. Until the late 1700s, New England meetinghouses had turned their long sides to the road with the main entry in the center, just as houses did. The minister's pulpit stood on the wall opposite the door.

This houselike plan was a Puritan innovation. Along with the spurning of saints' day, crosses, and vestments, Puritans rejected the traditional design of churches in England and elsewhere in Europe, which were long and narrow buildings, entered at the gable end and focusing all eyes on the altar. But starting in the 1790s, New Englanders reoriented many existing meetinghouses, turning their gable ends to the road, and built virtually all new ones on this pattern.

Beginning in 1836, the great clock in the Meetinghouse of the First Church in Belfast, Maine, kept the time for the village—as it does still. This view inside the Belfast church tower gives us a look at the massive mechanism of the tower clock.

As the Episcopal Church gained a foothold in New England, it sometimes built structures that sought to resemble more traditional English forms. But this one, the Trinity Episcopal Church in Brooklyn, Connecticut, is a purely New England structure, with elements of both meetinghouse and dwelling house.

(above) The interior view of the Alna meetinghouse in Alna, Maine, shows its well-preserved traditional high pulpit and square enclosed pews, which were already old-fashioned in 1800.

(right) With its Greek Revival trim and imposing steeple, this stylish meetinghouse set in the large and prosperous center village of the town of Dedham, not far from Boston, would have risen high above the other buildings in town.

The "church" form, once rejected on theological grounds, had become fashionable, and most congregations wanted up-to-date buildings. It was a sign of the softening of Puritanism to which almost no one objected. Meetinghouses also gradually became more churchlike and less severe in other ways. Stoves were introduced to warm congregations that had shivered through two-hour-long services. Church organs, pulpit hangings, and more elaborate interior woodwork softened the old austerity.

LEAVING NEW ENGLAND

By 1840 New England was producing textiles, shoes, clocks, and chairs for the rest of America, but its most important export was its people. Yankee schoolteachers and peddlers, along with New England books, could be found in every part of the country.

Large families and a limited supply of viable farmland meant that hundreds of thousands of New Englanders would leave their meetinghouses and rocky pastures for a pioneer life on the better lands of western New York and Ohio, and then on to northern Indiana, Illinois, and Michigan. In moving westward, New England ways merged and mixed with those of the new regions, and transplanted Yankees became a less provincial and peculiar people.

Many others in the region moved from countryside to villages or headed to Boston. Some of the most ambitious gathered up their belongings and boarded the stage or the railway car that would take them south to New York City, the emerging center of the nation's economy. It was the same route that many foreign visitors would take—and is the next step on our journey.

The first synagogue in New England, Touro Synagogue, Congregation Jeshuat Israel, in Newport, Rhode Island, was completed in 1763. Connecticut minister Ezra Stiles attended the dedication of "an edifice the most perfect of the Temple kind perhaps in America and splendidly illuminated." In contrast to its severe exterior, the interior of the Touro Synagogue is richly decorated.

THE

MIDDLE STATES

ALL IN A HURRY

Arriving in New York from New England would have been a shock, especially if you had never traveled outside of New England before. From your schoolbooks or the weekly newspaper you would have known a little about life in the Middle States, as New York, New Jersey, Pennsylvania, Maryland, and Delaware were called. But nothing in the world could have prepared you for New York City.

Where New England was sober, pious, homogeneous, and predictable, New York was all noise, activity, and motion—a whirlpool of motion, a sea of faces, a Babel of languages. And if it wasn't the loudest, fastest place on earth, it was as close to it as you'd ever been. New Yorkers, you quickly learned, lived and worked faster than the rest of the country.

New York was a city of many tongues and Americans of all religions (including some of none) from every part of the country, from all of the British Isles, and from most countries of Europe. Walking down the Broad Way or one of the city's other busy streets, you would hear English in several different accents, a good bit of Dutch, and conversations in German, French, Spanish, and Italian, and occasionally a more exotic tongue.

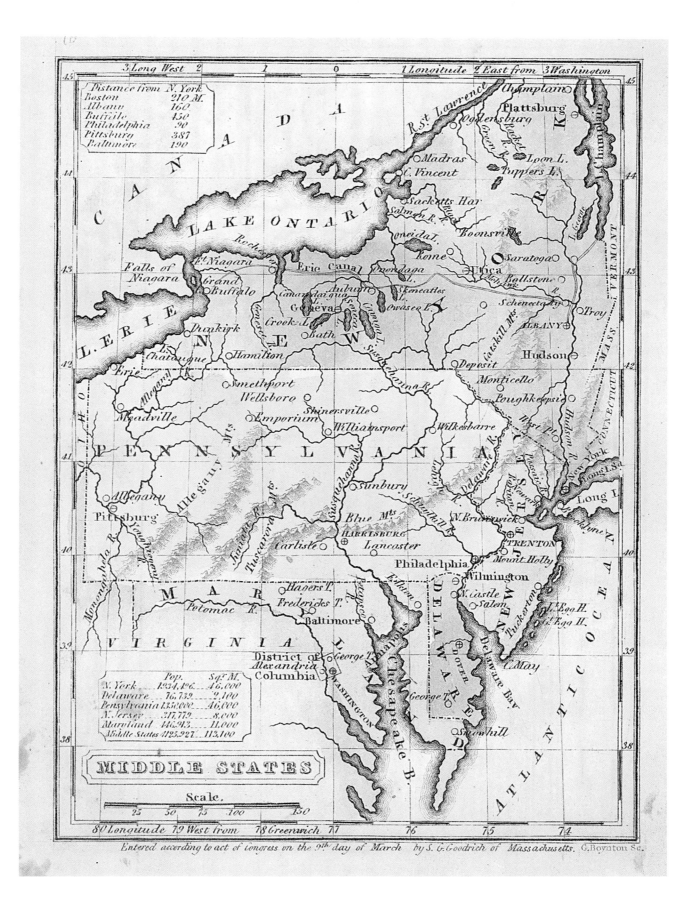

Built in 1841, this is the third Methodist church on John Street in Manhattan. The first was a small rough stone chapel of 1768; as the Methodists increased in numbers and prosperity, they built a larger church in 1818. As the city continued to grow, so did the congregation. The third church was this massive urban temple with a huge Palladian window over the entrance.

ON THE STREETS OF NEW YORK

The first of May was the city's "moving day" for its huge population of renters because almost all the leases expired at the end of April. It was a day of literal chaos on the streets. Frances Trollope was there in 1831 and saw hundreds of "packers, porters and draymen" moving furniture in open carts and wagons, creating enormous horse-drawn traffic jams, as well as poorer families moving their goods on wheelbarrows.

Eighty feet wide and more than two miles long, Broadway, or "the Broad Way," as New Yorkers called it, was "the great and fashionable resort for citizens and strangers." In good weather it was thronged. Pearl Street, which runs through lower Manhattan down to the Battery, was a "scene of great bustle and business . . . almost entirely occupied with stores and counting-houses," John Fowler wrote in 1831. Wall Street was already thick with bankers and brokers.

Although activity in the city rarely let up, New York had its great tides of daily activity. "Soon after sunrise," Theodore Dwight observed, came floods of dock workers, house builders, craftsmen, and laborers, carrying their noon dinners in "convenient little tin-kettles." Then came the clerks who worked in the city's thousands of mercantile and financial firms. The youngest arrived first, to open the offices and start the fires, followed by more senior employees. An hour or so later arrived "their masters, who flow down with more dignity, but scarcely less speed, to the counting-rooms of the commercial streets." At the end of this tidal flow of workers came schoolchildren; crowds of adults "crossed and mingled with some of the fourteen thousand children who go to the public and primary schools at nine." In the 1830s some observers guessed that at least 20,000 people came in and out of the city every day.

In the winter, Dwight rose in the early morning to watch the smoke begin to rise from the city's thousands of chimneys and wrote a compelling visual image of New York as it started up. It began with the houses of "five or ten early risers" in the upper part of the city, getting ready for work. Soon after, "their example is so contagious, that fires are speedily blazing in every house." On very cold days, these wood and coal fires produced a heavy pall of smoke that hung over the city. When the wind was blowing from the south, the Battery at the tip of Manhattan could be in brilliant sunlight, while the rest of the city was "deeply obscured" by smoke.

The city's traffic was dangerous to the unwary. Carts and freight wagons rumbled throughout the day, moving goods around the city. The public transit system—large horse-drawn passenger wagons called "omnibuses"—clogged the streets in the early morning and late afternoon.

(top) A circa 1830 house was located in Brooklyn, New York, then a separate, flourishing smaller city across the East River.

(bottom) Built around 1830, these Grove Street row houses are what would have been called "respectable tradesman's houses." They are 22 ft. by 32 ft. with six rooms on three floors.

Peter Neilson thought that "almost every house" in the city was "occupied by one family, and there is a back yard, less or more, attached to each house." But these were the lives and houses of the city's comfortable classes that he saw. Early censuses show that more New Yorkers lived in multiple-family houses than anywhere else in the early United States, a statistic that remains unchanged.

New York had "a few low quarters," where everything was dirty and poor, Andrew Bell noted, although he didn't seem impelled to investigate further. Yet he scoffed at travelers who claimed to have seen no serious poverty in the city. Bell had seen "scores of destitute homeless wretches lying on bulks, or under the sheds about the markets of New York," and wrote that he had "been an eye-witness to great misery, from cold and hunger, in the severe winter of 1835–6," with some people even dying in the streets.

One New York neighborhood, "Five Points," was infamous as a place where travelers didn't want to go unescorted—or unarmed. Charles Dickens saw it in 1840. ". . . In respect of filth and wretchedness," Five Points was as bad as any of London's worst. In her *Letters from New-York* in the early 1840s, the writer and reformer Lydia Maria Child described "A dilapidated building, in a filthy and crowded street," and an immensely crowded house occupied by 15 different families. "In the corner of one room, on a heap of rags, lay a woman with a babe three weeks old, without food or fire."

This leaky house, where "the wind whistles through and through, and the rain comes driving in," was a stunning contrast to "the princely mansions of Broadway."

THE DUTCH OF NEW YORK

Out of New York City to the north winds the Hudson River and its beautiful valley, sprinkled along the way on both sides with towns large and small, many of which in the early 1800s still bore the imprints of the Dutch. All of New York City and much of its surrounding land, including

East Hampton was in good part a cultural extension of Connecticut with houses in the characteristic New England form.

An ancient Dutch house sits in the midst of downtown Albany in the 1930s. "Said to be the oldest house in the city," noted the surveyors, but "no authentic information available." It certainly was very old, dating perhaps to the mid-1600s.

Places of Worship

"There is hardly a creed in Europe, that has not a society in the Middle States."
—*Pictorial Geography,* 1840

The religious diversity of the Middle States startled observers who came from more homogeneous places. Without quite intending it, the region became the nation's laboratory for pluralism and tolerance. Across the landscape could be seen Catholic churches and Quaker meetinghouses, Presbyterian churches and Methodist chapels, houses of worship for Episcopal, Dutch Reformed, German Reformed, Lutheran, and Baptist congregations.

There were synagogues in New York City, Philadelphia, and Baltimore, and meetinghouses for religious liberals—Unitarians and Universalists—who stretched the boundaries of Christian orthodoxy. And, from German-descended Moravians to largely English-descended Shakers, there were religious societies whose beliefs led them to separate from the world and create separate communities.

TOP: *The steeple of Christ Lutheran Church, built from 1812 to 1814, rises in York, Pennsylvania.* BOTTOM LEFT: *Constructed in 1685, this church was built in the Dutch style for its Dutch-speaking Hudson Valley Reformed congregation in Tarrytown, New York. It later became known as the "Sleepy Hollow" church, from Washington Irving's famous story.* BOTTOM CENTER: *The spire of this 1761 German Lutheran church was added in 1794, as were its remarkable hand-carved wooden statues of the Four Evangelists.* BOTTOM RIGHT: *This rear view of the church shows us the Dutch graveyard—and the unusual pentagon shape of the building.*

Long Island, parts of Connecticut, parts of New Jersey, and much of up-state New York, had been the province of *Nieuw Amsterdam.*

Descendants of Dutch settlers, some of whom had come from Flanders or from Protestant communities in France, held onto their language and customs in communities that took generations to fully move over to English ways. (Martin Van Buren, president from 1836 to 1840, was born in the Kinderhook near Albany. He grew up speaking Dutch and used it within his family; during his presidency, it was spoken in the family quarters of the White House.)

The New York countryside was also an area of some competition between the settled Dutch "Yorkers" and the "Yankees" who moved out of Connecticut into New York looking for more farmland. Washington Irving capitalized on this long-running conflict in his *Knickerbocker's History of New York* and, most unforgettably, in "The Headless Horseman."

"What uncomfortable neighbors this restless tribe must have been," Irving wrote, describing the feeling of the local Dutch toward the New Englanders who had pushed their way into New York, grabbing up land. Dutch farm families simply wanted to "go along in life just as their fathers and grandfathers had." For Irving, this was a confrontation between easygoing Dutchmen, who focused on farm, family, and town, and the ambitious, talkative, calculating Yankees, who were eager for change, profit, and improvement. This was a caricature, but it had an element of truth.

One New Englander, Sarah Kemble Knight, visited New York in the early year of 1704 (the Dutch had handed the city over to the British only 40 years earlier) and found the houses there "not altogether like ours in Boston." Dutch brick and tile made a sharp contrast with the all-wood houses of New England. She admired their glazed brick-work, noting that they were of "diverse coullers and laid in Checkers" and looked "very agreeable."

Inside, her housekeeper's eye noted that the houses she visited were "neat to admiration," with all their woodwork smoothly planed and scoured so that it was "kept very white." In one house, "the hearths were laid with the finest tile that I ever see, and the staircases laid all with white tile which is ever clean, and so are the walls of the Kitchen which had a Brick floor."

Later travelers revealed a variety of opinions on the Dutch. Suggesting generations of English-Dutch competition and warfare around the world, the Irish writer Isaac Weld thought the New York Dutch "very excellent farmers," although they had "inherited all

(top) A stone one-and-a-half-story farmhouse; a three-room plan with three doors, an upper story freight door, and an exterior oven.

(bottom) Kitchen interior, showing fireplace and hearth, in the Harden-bergh House in Kerhonkson, N.Y.

(above) Built in the 1760s in Albany County, New York, this stone house has a symmetrical facade in the English manner but has Dutch windows and a low gable.

(right) The floor plan of the Hardenbergh Dutch farmhouse shows its three front doors.

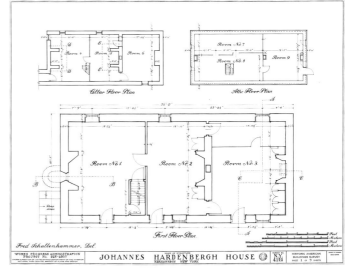

end so large or particularly heavy things could be hoisted up or down without squeezing through the narrow stairs.

Even prosperous Dutch farmers lived in these rambling single-story houses. They lived comfortably but without impressive façades, entryways, and stair halls, or symmetry—which is exactly what bothered New Englanders like Dwight. For this opinionated Yankee, domestic order and decency meant two-story houses, symmetry, regularity, and privacy. Dwight seems to have seen these simple Dutch farmhouses as peasant houses, where people lived without control over who came in and out of the house. Clearly, this was a violation of the order of things.

From the Dutch point of view, New Englanders valued only the façade. A Yankee family would build "a huge palace of pine boards" full of symmetrically placed windows and large enough by Dutch standards "for a parish church." But these wooden houses were "rickety" and their interiors weren't really comfortable.

Yet by the early 1800s, the New England model of home had clearly won. New York's cities came to be constructed "in the English manner," and Dutch farm families began to build houses that were versions of the Federal central-hallway plan and later of the Greek Revival plan.

IN THE WESTERN PARTS

Many New York houses would have been difficult to distinguish from New England ones. With their early settlement and high birth rates, Yankees had a head start on populating the nation's northern corner, and they moved both west and south in large numbers. Eastern Long Island was largely settled from Connecticut, and its houses, meetinghouses, and schools were essentially the same. New Englanders poured into New York from Connecticut and came across the Berkshires from western Massachusetts.

New Englanders and their descendants came to account for an increasingly large proportion of the state's population—as many as one-third, it was estimated in the 1830s. The towns and farming communities of western New York, settled since 1800, contained few surprises to travelers coming from the east. They had already seen New England.

Western New York also heavily bore the stamp of the Greek Revival. This reflected in part an upsurge of interest in the histories of the Greek and Roman republics, seen as ancient historical models for the new American nation. Nearly 200 New York towns founded after 1790 got Greek or Roman names—Troy, Syracuse, Homer, Utica, Cato, Cicero,

(top) Built in 1835 in Chautaugua County, New York, this "full-dress" Greek Revival house is completely framed by Ionic pilasters and Ionic columns.

(bottom) This central hallway house was built in 1802 in Madison County, New York.

Hector, Virgil. A lot of the children born there, especially the boys, got these names as well—Horace, Cyrus, Hiram, Lucius. After 1820, white-painted, temple-front, side-hall houses became western New York's architectural signature.

Although Frances Trollope criticized nearly everything about the new United States, she loved the New York community of Canandaigua, "as pretty a village as man ever contrived to build." She even temporarily set aside her English disdain for wooden houses. Canandaigua's temple-front houses and its Congregational meetinghouse were "so neatly painted, and in such perfect repair" that they were irresistibly attractive to her.

❋ EVERYDAY LIFE ❋

Schools

"The means of education are not neglected in some of the Middle States . . . it is not common, except among the foreigners and their children, to find a person who cannot read and write."

—*Pictorial Geography,* 1840

The Middle States were in between in many ways. They spanned a range—going north to south—between the nearly universal schooling of New England and the haphazard arrangements and significant illiteracy of the South. New Englanders, who always had the most to say about this, praised New York for its publicly supported schools but criticized Pennsylvania's patchwork of privately supported schools, arguing that education there was "backward" and that fewer than half of the state's children were in school.

LEFT: *A number of schoolhouses in the Middle States were built on this octagonal plan—one that maximized available space for pupils and the number of windows.* CENTER LEFT: *This stone schoolhouse was built in 1838. Many schoolhouses were probably much flimsier.* CENTER RIGHT: *Built in 1784 in East Hampton, New York, this is a large and substantial academy building in the New England style.* RIGHT: *This monumental structure was an expression of educational and social reform. It was built in 1833 as a free private school for "indigent youths" of Baltimore.*

In Hudson County, New Jersey, this is a small 21-ft. by 26-ft. frame side-hall house, circa 1840, on a small city lot. It has two rooms on each floor.

Not everything, of course, could be in perfect repair, and sometime ambitious Americans built beyond their means. A decade earlier, the Englishman Peter Stansbury passed through the central New York village of Montgomery and found something to smile at, though not admire.

The people of Montgomery badly wanted what Stansbury called "improvement and grandeur in the style of their buildings." They built numerous "large and fashionable" houses but neglected some important details. There were carpenters enough, but housepainters and glaziers to repair broken windows were nowhere to be found. From his point of view, the result was a joke—a community of almost new houses in bad repair. "The fine mouldings and window-shutters" went unpainted and were "stained with iron rust from bolts and heads of nails." When a window broke, it would be "carefully fastened up with shingles and pine boards, giving the whole edifice a very admirable regularity in its appearance."

The best, or worst, of all was a three-story house that had 16 windows across the front, along with others at the rear and on the gable ends. Its occupants found it "rather too expensive to keep in repair" and gradually closed each window with boards as it broke. When Stansbury arrived, he saw only one open window left in the building, where light came in "through five solitary remaining panes."

THE MIDDLE OF THE MIDDLE

New Jersey was the middle of the Middle States, and most people passing through it got no clear sense of its identity, which actually was various and complex. Anticipating common opinion today by nearly 200 years, a lot of people saw New Jersey as merely a corridor between New York City and Philadelphia. The Scotsman Andrew Bell saw things that way. In 1838, he passed through New Jersey on the brand-new railroad that connected the two cities and grumbled that it went through "as uninteresting a country as it was ever my fate to travel on."

Bell saw virtually no houses, only "woods of a mean character, growing in a light sandy soil," and small "dram shops" that sold drinks to the passengers when the train stopped for fuel and water. Unfortunately, he could have seen little more from the train because the railway passed through New Jersey's outer coastal plain, its least fertile and most thinly settled area. Another traveler, James Stuart, saw only "a flat and uninteresting country" on his way to Trenton, "though there are here and there some thriving little villages." He noticed an alternation of "thick woods" and "open country, covered entirely with fields of Indian corn.

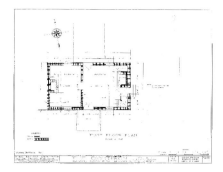

(left) The John and Mary Dickinson House, built in 1754, is likely the most spectacular example of Lower Alloways ornamental brickwork.

(top) A drawing of the Dickinson House shows that it measured 34 ft. by 20 ft. and had a two-room plan on each floor.

(bottom) This 1840s woodcut shows Newark, New Jersey, as a large and thriving commercial village, not yet a manufacturing city.

(above) The decorated houses of Lower Alloways are unusual because their front façades are far less visually striking than their ornamented end walls. With its two chimneys, this house has a two-room downstairs plan.

(right) An interior view of the first-floor room shows the fireplace, the winder stair going up to the chamber, and steps leading down to the cellar.

Yet had these folks ventured farther into New Jersey, they would have had a different opinion. Its territory had once been settled by Swedes and Finns, who had given way to the Dutch, who in their turn had given way to English rule. By the 1800s, the traces of Scandinavian settlement were a historical whisper, reflected in community names like Swedesboro and, perhaps, the architecture of a few surviving cabins built with round logs and notched corners.

East Jersey was in the orbit of New York and many of its people were descended from Dutch settlers and New England migrants, so the forms of their houses reflected this. West Jersey, in the orbit of Philadelphia, was originally settled from the West of England and dominated at first by Quaker families. One way to understand this distinctive part of the New Jersey landscape is to look carefully at a single community and its remarkable houses.

THE MONOGRAMMED HOUSES OF LOWER ALLOWAYS CREEK

The farming community of Lower Alloways Creek in Salem County, the southernmost part of New Jersey, was settled by Quakers from the West of England at the end of the 1600s. Farmers raised wheat and took produce when they could to Philadelphia, about 50 miles up the Delaware River.

Yet for years Lower Alloways Creek appears to have hidden from the rest of the world. No traveler before 1840 seems ever to have written about visiting it. There are no extensive accounts of life there. The 1798 Direct Tax schedules survive for the township, plus 10 houses from Alloways were documented by a Federal survey team in the 1930s. So with not much of a written record, the remarkable houses of Lower Alloways Creek must speak for themselves. What story do they tell?

The tax schedules tell us that Alloways, like most places in America at the time, had a strikingly unequal landscape of houses. Most of Alloways' best houses were two-story brick structures, and they naturally belonged to the most prosperous farmers. Five out of six of its 180 or so houses were frame or log structures, and many of them were worth only a few dollars. Half of its houses were less than 20 ft. by 24 ft., or smaller than a typical two-car garage. Some houses were as tiny as 14 ft. by 16 ft., the size of a standard master bedroom. And remember, entire families, often numbering up to a dozen, lived in these cramped places.

In a second snapshot taken more than a century later, HABS images give us another view of life in Alloways. They picture the brick

IN THEIR OWN WORDS

VOICES OF PHILADELPHIA

Henry Cogswell Knight recorded some of the public voices of the city. In Philadelphia's great central marketplace, a half mile of shops and stalls, thousands came every day to buy "flesh, fish, and fruit." There he heard the cries of the vendors: " 'pepper pot, right hot'; 'hot corn, hot corn'; 'oys, oys, poor Jack wants his money for selling pickled oysters.' " Late at night, he heard the watchmen making their rounds, calling out "past eleven o'clock, and a cloudy night" or "three o'clock, and a bright star-light" and "thus to strike the slow-passing note of time, through all the weary watches of their walks."

Built between 1832 and 1834 and designed by Philadelphia architect William Strickland, the Merchants' Exchange was a temple of business in the highest Greek Revival style. It became the center of Philadephia's mercantile trade, insurance and banking, and housed the city's central post office as well.

The first houses in Philadephia's Elfreth's Alley were built in 1713, the last in 1836. It has been called "America's oldest residential street."

Friends Meetinghouse, with its separate entrances for men and women and movable central partition. They show two log houses and fragments of a third.

By far the most striking images are of five two-story brick houses, which would have been the homes of Lower Alloways' leading families in the mid and late 1700s. Each one has an otherwise blank and windowless gable end elegantly decorated with patterned brickwork. We can literally "read" these exteriors because they proclaim the year of their building and the initials of their first owners, husband and wife.

This distinctive local tradition ensured that some mark of their builders' identities would remain, through all changes in ownership, as long as they stood. They remind us that each house embraced a household, and they memorialize the wife as well as the husband—a mark of the Quaker way, which gave women more honor and visibility.

We can also read the interior plans of these houses, which are very similar. Each one has a winding corner staircase and a front door that opens directly into the main living space—without an entry hall. Four have two sizable rooms on the first floor and two or three upstairs. One house is even more open; it has only a single large room on the first floor and another on the second. A New Englander would have been shocked to find prosperous families living with so little privacy.

PHILADELPHIA, QUAKERS, AND EXTREME ORDER

Visitors would complain about getting lost in Boston and New York's "crooked and diagonal streets." Visitors to Philadelphia would complain about too much uniformity. Philadelphia's streets "are so much alike and placed at such equal distances apart" that strangers often got lost because they couldn't tell one street from another, Peter Neilson of Glasgow wrote in 1828.

That neatness and sense of order had its roots in the Quakers, or members of the Society of Friends, who as a group largely settled in Pennsylvania and West Jersey. Quakers were religious radicals who, like New England Puritans, came to escape persecution in America, where they sought to purify Christian belief and practice. But they were a gentler people than the New Englanders. Refusing to participate in violence and seeking peace and order in their families and communities, Quakers emphasized the individual experience of God (they called it the "Inner

(top) These five three-story houses with dormer attics on Girard Row, built 1831-36, are an example of housing for prosperous tradesmen and storekeepers.

(above) A marble fireplace ornaments the parlor of a comfortable house on Girard Row, built in the early 1830s.

(left) Probably built by John Drinker, a bricklayer, circa 1760, this is a very small city house, with one room on each floor.

These four-story brick townhouses were built from 1835 to 1839. They were the typical houses of the city's most economically successful families.

Light") over the Bible. They abolished the pagan names of the days and months in favor of "First Day, First Month," etc., and avoided ritual in their often silent worship.

The great city they founded at the confluence of the Delaware and Schuylkill rivers reflected Quaker ways and values yet also managed to be a great center of commerce, finance, and manufacturing. Philadelphia didn't look like much from the water because its best buildings were out of sight. All that was visible from the river were ships, docks, wharves, and warehouses. But once they entered the city and walked its wide brick sidewalks, visitors were always struck by the city's simple orderliness.

In public life, Philadelphians were quieter than New Yorkers and more cautious in their business dealings, Neilson thought. Even non-Quakers had "received a considerable tinge of Quakerism, at least in appearance."

The New Englander Henry Cogswell Knight observed the city closely when he spent time there in 1814. It was "an immense chequer-board," he thought. The streets going east and west were numbered—as were the Quaker days and months. Those running north and south were "called after the trees in the vicinity—cedar, mulberry, sassafras, vine, chestnut, walnut, spruce, and pine." All nice, neat, and orderly, in the Quaker way of things.

Along with uniformity, in the "better streets" at least, went obsessive outdoor cleanliness. "The Philadelphians are a neat folk," wrote Knight. At least the city's prosperous families were. On Saturday evenings, household servants were "out before the front-door, to sweep the flag-stones, and bricked sidewalks, for the Sabbath." Frances Wright saw "the domestics of each house" washing their steps every morning—"a piece of outdoor housewifery, by the way, which must be somewhat mischievous to the ladies' thin slippers," suggesting the slip-and-fall potential of wet, scrubbed stone.

HOUSES IN A ROW

Visitors admired the neat brick houses that were the majority of houses in Philadelphia. They were better built than those in Europe, and their bricks were "uncommonly well manufactured," Knight wrote. But the "city of regularity" was densely packed and its prosperous neighborhoods were a bit too regular for his tastes: "After you have walked one square, you have seen the whole." There was not enough variety in the houses or the streets "to relieve the eye, or arrest the fancy."

Naturally, given the Quaker nature of things, little in Philadelphia was gaudy or lavishly ornamented, which led Knight to conclude that

This meticulous drawing documents the façades, steps, windows, and doorways of the early houses of Elfreth's Alley in Philadelphia.

everything had been "quakerfied." In describing Philadelphia, he invoked Thomas Paine, who said, "If a Quaker had been consulted at the Creation," the world would have come out in shades of gray and brown. Still, he thought Philadelphia "a noble city; wealthy, substantial, convenient." In short, it was a good place to live for its thousands of comfortably off families.

Orderliness and regularity were the most common themes of travelers' descriptions. They admired the overall effect, but nothing distinctive caught their eyes. Andrew Bell, a Scotsman who visited in the late 1830s, acknowledged that most of the city's houses were well built but thought "the general result is the most wearisome uniformity imaginable."

The houses, said Gideon Miner Davison's *Guide to the Middle and Northern States*, were

---

✹ EVERYDAY LIFE ✹

Taverns

"The taverns are of all kinds, from mere hovels to large hotels."

—*Pictorial Geography*, 1840

"Every ten or twelve miles upon this road there are taverns, which are all built of wood . . . with a porch in front the entire length of the house. Few of these taverns have any signs, and they are only to be distinguished from the other houses by the number of handbills pasted up on the walls near the door." —Isaac Weld, 1795, traveling through Maryland

"I do not suppose that it is possible to arrive at any very exact estimate of the taverns in this country," James Fenimore Cooper wrote. "A vast number are very bad." In the largest cities some taverns became true hotels,

which served lavish meals and offered private rooms for the most fastidious travelers. Another institution for strangers was also arising there, the boardinghouse—a place where single men and even married couples could live for months on end, paying for both food and lodging.

Travelers soon discovered that the farther from the city and the more impassable the road, the worse they fared. Given the scattered nature of American settlement and the great distances that had to be traveled, this was inevitable. In fact, the only tiresome thing about these otherwise fascinating accounts of early travelers is their endless complaints about tavern food and accommodations.

(above) A row of three small houses was built circa 1815 in the large village of York, Pennsylvania; the last house on the end is only one small room deep.

(right) In the attic of the Kaufman house in Berks County, Pennsylvania, rafters and collar beams surround the massive central chimney.

neat, "commodious" (comfortable), and uniform. Charles Daubney of Oxford noted that "it is curious to observe how nearly they all appear to be on the same plan, the difference betwixt them consisting chiefly in the greater or less size of the rooms." They had a first-floor plan of two parlors, one for dining and one for receiving company, kitchen below, and bedchambers above.

But other parts of the "city of regularity" were invisible to most travelers. Philadelphia had a lot of poor working families, white and black, living on the outskirts of these orderly squares—or worse, living next to the wharves. They also usually lived in the city's flimsier and smaller wooden houses in an environment that, unsurprisingly, was dirtier than the neat squares of the well off.

Philadelphia's famed physician Benjamin Rush noticed a connection between these cramped and filthy living conditions and the city's terrible yellow fever epidemic in 1793. Fifty years later, another physician, Isaac Parish, noted that the houses of the poor on Water Street lacked "yards, privies, or any means of ventilation." These families were too busy struggling for the necessities of life to wash their steps and sweep the pavement. Henry Cogswell Knight saw "half famished" chimney sweeps, barely clothed, looking for work on the city's streets.

When the Stiegel House in Lebanon County, Pennsylvania was demolished, it was discovered that underneath layers of siding was a German-style half-timbered house. This view shows its heavy timber frame, filled with clay "nogging."

PENNSYLFANISCH DEITCH,
OR THE PENNSYLVANIA GERMANS

Compared with the Quakers, Dutch, and especially New Englanders, Pennsylvania Germans were a separate people.

Lack of land and religious freedom in Europe drove them to America, where they were encouraged to settle in Pennsylvania, which—thanks to the Quakers—was the most open and tolerant of the British colonies. Beginning in the late 1600s, they came by the many thousands and they came ready to take up the land and work it.

The French botanist Andre Michaux gave them hearty praise in 1795 as he rode into eastern Pennsylvania in search of interesting plants. "The land better cultivated, the enclosures better formed, prove clearly it is a German settlement. . . . They assist each other in their harvests, live happy among themselves, always speak German, and preserve, as much as possible, the customs of their ancestors." More successfully than the New York Dutch, because their numbers were much larger, the Germans kept their language and traditions, including the old ways of building.

Germans weren't the only good farmers in Pennsylvania, of course. Americans of English, Scotch, Welsh, and Irish descent worked the same productive soil and produced grain, meat, butter, and cheese in such quantities that "the farms in general, in Pennsylvania, are considered as being in the best order of any in the Union," Isaac Holmes wrote in 1821. Still, the German presence on the land was distinctive and always remarkable.

BARNS FIRST, HOUSES LATER

Sensing that few Americans outside Pennsylvania knew anything about their German fellow citizens, Declaration of Independence signer Dr. Benjamin Rush wrote a short book in 1789 to enlighten them: "A German farm may be distinguished from the farms of the other citizens of the State," he explained, "by the superior size of their barns; the plain but compact form of their houses, the height of their inclosures; the extent of their orchards; the fertility of their fields; the luxuriance of their meadows, and a general appearance of plenty and neatness."

Their smaller houses, he went on, were "composed of a mixture, of wood, brick and clay, neatly united. The large houses are built of stone." German stone barns, often built before the family had moved out of its first log house, were the most impressive agricultural buildings anywhere in America.

The German traveler Johan Schoepf had already noted in 1783 that a Pennsylvania German house "could, even at a distance, be readily distinguished from one erected by a Scotch, Irish or Englishman." In Pennsylvania, virtually all houses with one central chimney, in *der Mitte des Hauses*, were German, following a plan that was long traditional in the region the settlers came from as opposed to houses with a chimney at each gable end, which were identifiably English.

Families often expected that their houses would follow a clear two- or three-generation pattern of improvement. The first house on a German farm, Rush said, was usually "small, and built of logs." It was expected to last the "life time of the first settler." The second generation would go on to build "a large and convenient stone house." He translated a German adage that said, "A son should always begin his improvements where his father left off." Rush oversimplified. Not all German families moved so easily into prosperity, and in a typical big family, the comfortable stone house could only be passed down to one child. Still, it was a noteworthy and fairly consistent pattern.

In 1818, the English agricultural writer William Cobbett noticed that on many eastern Pennsylvania farms the small log houses of the first

(top) An early English house built in 1683 and 1696. This is probably the earliest English-built house in Pennsylvania, as well as the only one known to have been visited by William Penn. It consists of two one room, stone sections with separate front doors.

(bottom) A sketch of this early house was published in 1843 in Sherman Mays' **Historical Collections of Pennsylvania.**

First Known Sketch of Caleb Pusey House - published in 1843
appeared in Sherman Mays Historical Collections of Pennsylvania
wrongly labeled as "Richard Townsend's Original Dwelling"

settlers remained alongside the larger and later stone houses: "The means, accumulated in the small house, enabled a son to rear the large one." Although he noted that "when pride enters the door, the small house is sometimes demolished," he hoped that many of them could be preserved as proof of the industry and virtue of the first generation.

Many German houses had three rooms on the first floor: *Stube, Kammer, und Kuche,* or public room, bedchamber, and a kitchen with the house's single fireplace. Like New York Dutch houses and many *English* ones in the southern parts of the Middle States, traditional German houses were entered directly from the road and often had two front doors. By the later part of the 1700s, however, the most prosperous German families were adopting some English ways. They started to build their houses "after the English fashion" with Georgian/ Federal symmetry and central hallways.

The Kaufman family built this large stone farmhouse in the 1760s. The smaller addition came in 1834.

(above) In 1795, a wealthy Berks County German family, the Spangs, decided to build this house "in the English manner."

(right) On the second floor of the Kaufman House, four open steps lead to a door and the closed stair-way to the attic.

A large German stone farm-house and barn are seen across the mill pond near Cocalico, in Lancaster County, Pennsylvania.

GERMAN PLAIN LIVING

German families had standards of home and standards of home comfort that were different from the English world. "The German farmers live frugally in their families, with respect to diet, furniture and apparel" and generally aspired only to "plain and useful" furniture instead of sofas, tea tables, and sideboards, Rush said. "They eat sparingly, of boiled animal food, with large quantities of vegetables, particularly sallad, turnips, onions and cabbage, the last of which, they make into Sourcrout. They likewise use a large quantity of milk and cheese in their diet."

He also noticed something interesting: that, for generations, these Germans kept their houses warmer in winter than other Americans. As "great economists of their wood," they used stoves for domestic heating long before they were adopted by the rest of the country. Their "large close stoves" made their houses so comfortable that in the winter German families could do twice the work of their neighbors who sat shivering around their open fireplaces. The English traveler William Priest admitted their comfort but disliked them on other grounds: "Close iron stoves" made houses too dry and were "terrible enemies to [the] beauty" of Pennsylvania's women.

Along with praise went criticism and sometimes ridicule. Germans were held up to mild derision in the *Pictorial Geography* because of the way they dressed. Men wore "broad-brimmed hats, and purple breeches," instead of the tall hats and tan, gray, or black pantaloons that men wore in Massachusetts and New York. And women's petticoats were "extremely short."

And they were different in another way—a difference that went against the grain of the English. German families saw nothing wrong with wives and daughters going into the fields to help with harvest. This surprised many English observers, but it shocked critical New Englanders like Dwight. In an earlier echo of a current debate, others criticized the Germans for maintaining their own language and not learning English.

The most unpleasant critique of the Pennsylvania Germans charged them with being overly materialistic. Isaac Holmes, who visited Pennsylvania in 1821, said the Germans were not only "extremely industrious" but greedy of gain. "The sums of money which some of them hoard are astonishing." Since just about all Americans were eager to make money, we can assume that Holmes was listening to other Pennsylvanians who were jealous of the frugal Germans' success.

(top) Here in the attic of the Brinton House, a 1704 English house in Delaware County, can be seen the rafters and collar beams with their corresponding builder's marks on them. Before raising a house frame, builders carefully matched and marked their timbers so that the complete frame would fit together.

(bottom) The lower-level kitchen of the Brinton House boasted an enormous stone fireplace.

The "Second Family" village, one of
the settlements of the Mount Lebanon
Shaker community, stands out starkly
in the rural New York landscape.

THE AMAZING SHAKERS

In both their architecture and their unique social organization, some of the most distinctive American communities were created by the "United Society of Believers in Christ's Second Coming," universally called the Shakers. They had been founded by "Mother Ann" Lee, a religious visionary who came to New York in 1774 with a small group of followers from Manchester, England. Mother Ann was hailed as a second Christ, a female incarnation of the Deity; she proclaimed celibacy and communal life for her followers. By the early 1800s, the Shakers, despite initial persecution, had claimed many converts, and there were numerous Shaker villages across the country from Maine to Kentucky.

Supporting themselves by communal farming and handcrafts, growing only by the admission of converts, and worshiping in ways that outsiders thought extremely eccentric, the Shakers soon became an American tourist attraction, often allowing visitors to observe their way of life and religious services. Visiting a Shaker village became a "must see" stop on tours of America.

Coming first to New England and rural New York, the Shakers built largely in the fashion of New England, with mostly frame houses sided in clapboards and a few brick and stone structures. Shaker agriculture was productive, their garden seeds were widely sold, and the quality of their workmanship was widely admired. Their offices, shops, and communal houses were strictly unornamented in a style that many observers thought bore a severe elegance.

"Their buildings are very clean looking within and without," James Stuart wrote after visiting the largest Shaker community, in New Lebanon, New York, in 1832. "They are large, plain and handsome— almost all painted of a yellowish colour." The houses and farms—everything in and around Shaker communities—were amazingly neat, without litter, refuse, or even weeds.

Andrew Bell was impressed by the New Lebanon Trustees' House, where the male and female elders of the community lived in separate apartments. It was "a substantially-built and very neat structure, two

(top) Built in 1824, this was the
primary place of worship for Mount
Lebanon, New York, the largest of
the Shaker communities.

(bottom) The Watervliet or Neskayuna,
New York, Shaker community was
another one frequently visited by
travelers. Its First Meetinghouse was
built in 1791.

Homewood

On the outskirts of Baltimore, between 1801 and 1803, a great house was being built. It was being financed by Charles Carroll of Carrollton, the wealthy planter, statesman, and signer of the Declaration of Independence, for his son, Charles Carroll Jr. Yet the elegance and order of Homewood's architecture (it is now part of the Johns Hopkins University campus) contrasted sharply with the often acrimonious correspondence between father and son about its construction.

"You must keep separate accounts with your carpenter, brick-maker, stone-mason and brick-layer," admonished the father, afraid that his son would not control construction costs. The younger Carroll was already running up huge bills for carriages, horses, and furniture, which his father warned him to "cease and put a stop to."

A few months later, Carroll Sr. complained about "extravagant expenditures on your buildings" and that "vast sums have been squandered." In 1803 he exploded in exasperation. "The building of Homewood . . . will not fall short of $40,000," he wrote, which was a sum equivalent to millions in today's dollars. The great house with its many outbuildings was "a most improvident waste of money, and which you will have reason to look back on as long as you live with painful regret."

Yet he was an indulgent father who paid all the bills for a remarkable house that father and son created—more or less—together.

This early nineteenth-century engraving shows Shakers dancing during a service.

stories high; such a place as would be fit for the residence of an English gentleman of moderate fortune." Shaker interiors of whitewashed walls, built-in drawers, and racks of pegs for hanging garments struck him as "a model of order and comfort."

Shaker worship, on the other hand, struck him as extremely strange. He was one of a crowd of spectators in the New Lebanon meetinghouse who watched a Sabbath-day service: Two opposing lines of men and women repeated the verses of Shaker songs while moving back and forth, "sometimes in circles, at other times in ellipses; one while the brothers stood still and let the sisters whirl round them; otherwhiles the reverse; but however the figure changed, there was never any commingling of sexes." Men and women kept their arms close to their bodies and beat time with their hands "to the quick measure of their song."

The Big House of Faith

The Englishman William Newnham Blane enjoyed his stay in Baltimore in 1831 and looked carefully at the city's Catholic Cathedral, America's first. It had been designed by Benjamin Latrobe, the architect of the U.S. Capitol, and was widely considered then, as now, as one of the nation's finest neoclassical buildings.

But he was unable to admire it. It might have been, he admitted, that he preferred the Gothic style

Built in 1821, this Greek Revival church was the first Roman Catholic cathedral in the United States, designed by Benjamin Latrobe, the architect of the U. S. Capitol.

for churches. Or it might have been because he disapproved of how it was built. The cathedral's construction had in part been funded by a lottery, which Blane considered "might induce a heretic to suppose that the builders were at the same time serving both God and mammon."

It is only fair to note that college buildings across the United States, as well as Boston's Bunker Hill Monument, were financed in the same way.

(top) This two-room stone house in Cecil County, Maryland, has a gambrel-roofed frame addition and a remarkable name for so unpretentious a structure: "Success."

(left) Another Maryland house with a striking name, "Industry", in St. Mary's County, is a story and a half, probably with a two-room plan. It has a dramatic double chimney stack; its freestanding kitchen is close by.

Rose Hill in Charles County, Maryland, is a substantial tobacco plantation house of the late 1700s, frame with brick ends, two symmetrical brick wings, and four dramatic chimneys. The men in the picture appear to be admiring it.

(top) Possibly from the late 1600s, this one-story-and-a-loft house in Sussex County, Delaware, has a timber frame filled with brick and is clapboarded. Its floor plan is a single large room, 20 ft. by 30 ft.

(bottom) Look carefully and you'll see that this modest size one room house has a carefully detailed course of dentil decoration under the eaves.

ON THE SOUTHERN EDGE: MARYLAND AND DELAWARE

If Puritans had gone to New England and Quakers to Pennsylvania so they could worship God as they saw fit, so too had some of England's persecuted Catholics gone to Maryland, founded by the Catholic Cecil Calvert, Lord Baltimore. They did not long remain in the majority, but Maryland had the new nation's largest Catholic community.

Maryland had one of the nation's great cities, a diverse blend of peoples and faiths, and features of landscape and architecture that united it with eastern Pennsylvania, Delaware, and West Jersey. Like their Pennsylvania neighbors, the farmers of Maryland grew wheat and corn.

Yet in Maryland, the world of the Middle States blended with the world of the Southern States. Maryland was also a slave state, with a plantation economy still partly based on tobacco and families that made great fortunes on the land and built great houses. (By 1800, slavery was on its way to disappearing from Pennsylvania and states to the north; by the 1820s it was virtually extinct.)

Crossing the border from Pennsylvania into Maryland, travelers saw a different world. Elias Pym Fordham noticed that the people of Maryland were "a different people." In Pennsylvania, "white people are seen working in the fields and roads," he wrote in 1817. In Maryland he saw only slaves. James Fenimore Cooper wrote that on "entering Maryland," he saw a "change for the worse in the appearance of the country" —a slovenliness in fences and fields that he attributed to habits bred in a slave society.

But white Marylanders were not exactly southerners. They were not really like Virginians, Elias Fordham said, after spending two weeks in their company. They were a mixed people, German, Irish, and English. Poorer Marylanders he found awkward and inquisitive to strangers on the road. The wealthy were polite but reserved.

Isaac Weld loved the scenery, the "bold and extensive prospects" of the Susquehanna and Chesapeake Bay, with "the waters of some little creek or rivulet rushing over ledges of rock in a beautiful cascade." But locals were immune to the charms of the landscape. To them, he said after traveling near Elkton in 1795, "the sight of a wheat field or a cabbage garden would convey pleasure far greater than the most romantic woodland views."

In 1744, Dr. Andrew Hamilton of Maryland passed through Delaware and liked what he saw. "The people all along the road were making of hay," he wrote in his diary, which gave "a very sweet and agreeable smell." It was good farming country, with meadows and pastures as good as he had seen when in England. "The country here is not hilly, nor are the woods very tall or thick."

Hamilton was unusual. Few travelers came to Delaware and left even the most scant description of one of the smallest state's people or land. The state had many farms, only a few slaves (4 percent of its population), and a handful of plantations. The whole population of Delaware was less than the population of Baltimore.

HOUSES ON THE SOUTHERN EDGE

The people of Delaware had "very neat brick houses upon their farms," Hamilton wrote. He probably also saw many far flimsier wooden houses but wouldn't have mentioned them.

(above) Shown here is the oldest part of a house, Breckrock, in Kent County, Delaware, with a complicated history. It began as a one-room, dirt-floored brick house in the late 1600s; the HABS surveyors noted that it was "built crudely and suggested haste." In the early 1700s, a wooden floor was laid and the walls were plastered. Additions came in the mid and late 1700s, making the house substantially more comfortable.

(right) This two-and-a-half-story house in Kent County, Maryland, has symmetrical chimneys but no central hall. Instead, there are two front doors and a small winder stair up to the second floor. There are two ordinary bedchambers on the second floor, and the dormer windows light a single open sleeping space.

This story-and-a-loft frame house in Prince George's County, Maryland, has one room or two very small rooms, as well as an exterior fireplace. It is similar to the small Maryland farmhouse that Frances Trollope visited in 1828.

In both Maryland and Delaware a few great houses and some very substantial ones would have been the most visible, but one- or two-room houses were the most common, especially houses that were 16 ft. or 20 ft. square with a separate kitchen of 10 ft. or 12 ft. square. Most farm families lived in houses with a chimney at one end and one first-floor room that was entered directly from the outside. Most houses had just a loft upstairs, reached by a ladder. Better houses had a one-room second story, reached by a winding corner staircase. Many were built of wood, and the very poorest had dirt floors and even lacked chimneys. The very best of them, although still small, were solid two-story brick houses with carefully applied ornamental details.

During her stay in Maryland, Frances Trollope kept seeing these small houses, often at the center of big farms. The contrast of a large, rich farm and a tiny farmhouse fascinated her: "I went into the houses and remained long enough, and looked and listened sufficiently, to obtain a tolerably correct idea of their manner of living." She spent an afternoon in a tiny two-room frame house that was attached to a 300-acre farm (this same size farm in Massachusetts, New York, or Pennsylvania would have meant a large two-story house). It belonged to a young husband and wife with two small children and three slaves. As she described the house, it couldn't have been much larger than 20 ft. by 12 ft. (240 sq. ft.). The main room, used for entertaining visitors and taking meals, was "about twelve feet square." The second room was "hardly larger than a closet; this second chamber was the lodging room of the white part of the family."

Looking up, she noticed that "above these rooms was a loft, without windows," which in such a little house would have been reached by a ladder. This, she was told, was where overnight visitors stayed. The building "looked as if the three slaves might have overturned it, had they pushed hard against the gable end."

As small as the house was, it wasn't quite as small as Mrs. Trollope's description suggests because the kitchen, following the typical practice south of Pennsylvania, was a separate building a little distance away. However, it was a "shanty, a black hole without any window," where the slaves—two young women and a boy—slept as well as cooked.

LORD BALTIMORE'S CITY

Baltimore was the fastest-growing city on the American Atlantic coast. In the 1750s, it had been a small and straggling settlement, with "only two brick houses, and a few wooden ones . . . scarcely deserving the name of a town," William Priest noted. By the 1790s, the flow of

(top) West St. Mary's Manor in St. Mary's County Maryland, has a striking profile. Like Rose Hill, it is of frame construction with brick ends and double chimneys, but it is lower on the landscape, with one and a half stories and a low gable roof.

(bottom) This view shows an almost perfectly preserved Baltimore retail storefront, circa 1835.

A Baltimore street of the early 1800s
shows houses of various sizes, façades,
and roof styles. The gritty street lacks
the regularity that impressed many
visitors to Baltimore, but it is more
interesting to the modern eye.

*(top) A street of early 1800s row
houses has its door at street level,
without stoops.*

*(bottom) An early frame house, likely
constructed before 1750, consists of
two small rooms and a loft. As it
survived into the later 1700s, its
frame architecture would have made
it fairly unusual. It would not have
been out of place farther south in
Maryland.*

commerce had given it some 20,000 inhabitants and made it, in William Loughton Smith's words, "a large, handsome place, containing a number of good brick houses and inhabited by several thriving and wealthy merchants."

By 1840, Baltimore had just over 100,000 people, ranking it with Philadelphia, New Orleans, and Boston as the nation's great cities behind New York. It was also the greatest market for flour in the United States and probably in the world.

Isaac Weld didn't like Baltimore houses. He called them "small, heavy and inconvenient." But he liked the people. "English, Irish, Scotch and French" were busily engaged in trade and were "mostly plain people, sociable . . . and very friendly and hospitable toward strangers."

Baltimore continued to develop the distinctive architecture of brick row houses that it shared with Philadelphia. Dwight wrote in 1834 that its "broad and straight streets are lined with large stores and houses, some of which rival in taste the best in the country, and are thronged with well-dressed and busy people."

PENNSYLVANIA AS THE WEST

Before you think we've left the Middle States without touring western Pennsylvania, I've put off Pittsburgh until we get to what was called the West. Still lightly settled, before 1840, in many ways, northern and western Pennsylvania really were part of America's West.

The stories of their houses, and of the city of Pittsburgh, are better told beside those of Ohio, Indiana, and Illinois. In their ethnic and religious diversity, their productive agriculture, and fast-growing commercial cities, the Middle States anticipated much of the American future.

Increasingly divided by slavery after 1800, they also foreshadowed conflict and division. Some travelers ventured westward from the Middle States to track the great tides of migration into the new states. Others continued southward, into the heart of a slave-holding society defined in white and black—a very different part of America.

THE SOUTH

*A row of slave quarters
at the McLeod Planta-
tion near Charleston, S.C.,
goes on into the distance.*

AT THE HEART OF THE SOUTH—SLAVERY

Describing the early American South is complex and thorny. White and black together were locked into a system that provided great wealth for some but, to a variety of degrees, injured everyone. To clearly see the South, we need to remember how entrenched slaveholding was, that many of the founding fathers owned slaves, and that most people in the North were willing to tolerate it. No one mourns the end of slavery. It was cruel and unjust and needed to come to an end. However, racism was close to universal among whites in the 1800s. African-Americans suffered an enormous and long-enduring wrong, which is visible even as we look at these old buildings. We can't understand the landscape of Southern houses and families unless we first look at slavery.

THE BOUNTY OF BONDAGE

Travelers marveled at the natural abundance of what Americans called the "Southern States," which traced an arc from Virginia along the Atlantic Coast to Louisiana on the Gulf of Mexico. Although the most common description of the climate was "hot, moist, and insalubrious"—or dangerous to the health—the long growing season meant that "the productions of nature exhibit the greatest luxuriance and variety" in the South, as the *Pictorial Geography* phrased it.

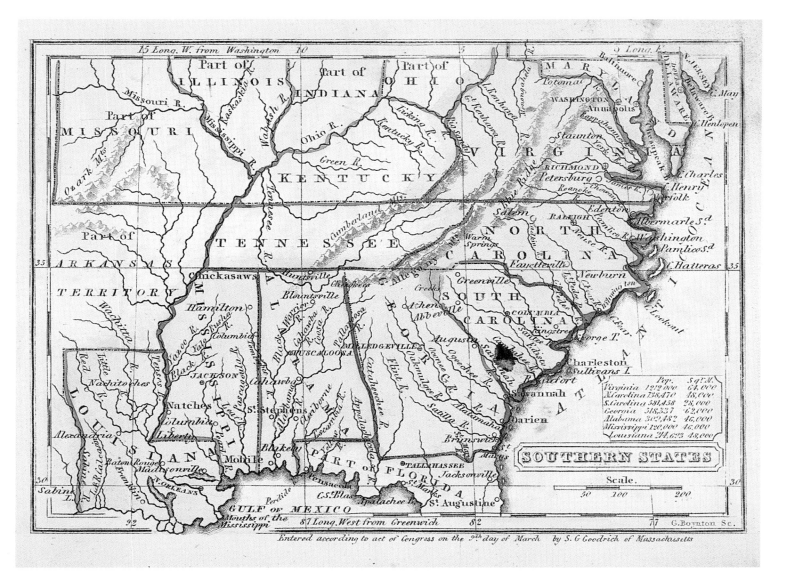

(top) This two-room log house was part of the slave quarters on the Will Crenshaw Plantation, built in the early 1800s.

(bottom) On the first floor of this town house in Charleston, South Carolina, sliding double doors within an ornate doorcase frame a view from one large drawing room into the next.

Farmers large and small throughout the country produced grain, meat, butter, cheese, and vegetables, which they consumed at home, sold in villages and cities, or sometimes exported. But in the South, real fortunes came to planters who used slave labor to grow the big cash crops of rice, indigo, sugar cane, tobacco, and cotton—products that entered the international economy on a large scale. Bound together, planters and slaves produced a bounty that made the United States the world's largest agricultural exporter. Before mid-century, plantation agriculture created most of America's wealthiest families.

The abundance came at a great price. Long before American independence, the South's prosperity and way of life depended completely on a vast labor force of black slaves (almost 40 percent of the Southern population) who cultivated and harvested the high-cash crops. Laws, customs, habits of mind, houses—the land itself—all were shaped by the demands of what Northerners called the "peculiar institution" of slavery.

It was the very climate of the South that gave the defenders of slavery an argument that a lot of people found plausible. "The Southern States, at least Georgia and the Carolinas, must be cultivated by blacks or abandoned," Elias Pym Fordham wrote in 1817. "The heat there is so excessive in August that to walk a mile in the Sun would subject a European to the most imminent danger." Many Americans embraced such "scientific" justifications to show why African-Americans could work safely in the blazing heat while whites couldn't.

HONOR, FAMILY, SLAVES

Travelers' descriptions of slave owners are remarkably consistent. They were more hospitable and generous than other Americans. They set greater store by family and their lives embraced a wider circle of kin than was true of Northeasterners. They valued personal independence and personal honor. And the wealthiest among them, the slaveholding planters at the head of this society, carried these qualities to the extreme. Planters had "more haughtiness, courtesy, and a higher estimation of personal dignity, than those of the North," Samuel Goodrich thought. As for the slaves, our observers simply could not comprehend their lives.

Slave owners weren't in the majority, but they were certainly a large and powerful minority. Across the South, almost one family in three owned at least one slave. In South Carolina and Mississippi, where blacks outnumbered whites, almost half the families owned slaves, although most owned just a few. Only a handful of families—2,000 at the most—lived on the great plantations that were the icons of the South's social order.

The past glory of the Anchuka plantation house can be seen even in its almost ruinous state. The house was built in about 1790 near Port Gibson, Mississippi, north of Natchez.

(top) These are the slave quarters
at Liberty Hall in Crawfordville,
Georgia.

(right) Built in Butler County,
Alabama, in the early 1800s, this
small one-story frame house was
raised up on ramshackle piers.

Yet most white Southerners didn't own slaves. Most were small-time farmers who might grow a little tobacco or cotton but more often grew corn and raised hogs. Some were the families of craftsmen, small store-keepers, teamsters, and stage drivers, but these were few. White overseers, who worked as managers on large plantations, also usually owned no slaves, although they were more deeply involved in the system than the average Southerner.

The truth was that if you were a success, you owned slaves and if you didn't, you didn't count for much in the eyes of the big plantation owners. The "poorer class of whites" or "inferior cultivators" (they had various names) were much maligned by most people who traveled the South, who little understood their ways or sympathized with their situation. "Those who have no slaves, are in some parts of a grade hardly above the slaves themselves," the *Universal Geography* maintained. That was a common view.

Many of these poor whites were illiterate and isolated, both literally and economically. They were called "foresters" because they emerged out of the woods to visit the store, the tavern, or the courthouse. Or "crackers" because they would crack their whips when riding their wagons into town. They certainly seem to have been hard drinking, rough, and sometimes violent. The poor Southern white had few defenders.

The aristocratic Margaret Hall, not surprisingly, found them exceptionally difficult, whether on the road or in the country taverns where she'd stopped. "The manners of the secondary classes are more disagreeable, gruff and boorish than anything I saw elsewhere." She accused them of "unbending frigid heartlessness." They could have accused her of arrogance. Caught between the slave owners and the slaves, they refused to be deferential to a demanding foreigner.

And although there were more of them, poor whites—dispersed, marginal, and unschooled—were not really in the majority at all. In every Southern state, nonslave-owning whites were substantially outnumbered by slaves and slaveholders taken together. However you choose to see them, they were on the outside.

LAND UNDER A SHADOW

When travelers described the South, they described both the reality in front of them and the not always visible but overshadowing presence of slavery. Slavery had "a sensible [perceivable] effect on the manners of the inhabitants," the Englishman Isaac Holmes wrote in 1822. He

(top) A striking story-and-a-half central-hall house, built in the 1770s, is typical of many Virginia plantation houses. Built in New Kent County, Virginia, it has since been moved to Williamsburg.

(bottom) This plantation house from Madison County, Alabama, has a Greek Revival facade of six massive brick pillars. Those who disliked the American fashion of wooden classical pillars couldn't complain.

An abandoned house near St. Brides in Chesapeake County, Virginia, has just traces of its chimneys left standing as evidence it ever existed.

thought that the "vigor of mind" that he had seen in New England contrasted sharply with the "listlessness and indolence" that he observed on the roads and in the taverns.

Travelers had a complicated response to the South. The scenery was often striking and beautiful, and they frequently found great courtesy and hospitality. But the roads were worse, the fences more often out of repair, and the houses not as well maintained.

In the homes of the wealthiest, "an air of lazy luxury pervades" because of the abundance of household slaves to carry on all domestic work, Elias Pym Fordham wrote. He found splendor in these great establishments but usually saw "little Comfort," by which he meant the signs of energetic cooking, housekeeping, and laundering.

Throughout the South, travelers saw a landscape of neglect. Because slavery devalued hard work, wealthy white Southerners often tended to neglect details of maintenance and housekeeping or left them to slaves, who had little motivation. Judging severely—as she always did— Margaret Hall saw inefficient taverns, unpainted houses, and bad roads as sure signs of economic failure. "There is not a single town or village through which we have passed south of Philadelphia which is not on the decay. From the moment the slave system commences, so does the decline." She was writing about Alabama in 1828.

She was wrong about the South's slave economy. It was thriving. Slavery was not a declining institution but an immensely profitable one. Plantation agriculture was expanding wildly into new lands, and great fortunes were being made. The sloppiness people saw was real, but it didn't mean economic decline. What it meant was a distribution of resources and a way of life that put less value on material orderliness.

The vast size of the South and the scattered nature of its towns made it impossible to take it in at a glance. In most places it was only partly cleared, a patchwork of woods and open fields. By leaving the main road and following a river or ridge, Henry Cogswell Knight often came to a plantation where he would find "a house and out-buildings, on a spot cleared in the middle of the woods." No ordinary farms with "fifteen or twenty acres of arable land" but "from one to five hundred" acres under intensive cultivation, "not tilled by five or six hired men, but by from thirty to one or two hundred slaves."

In the clutter of its dooryard, this gambrel-roofed house in King William County, Virginia evokes the rough texture of the Southern landscape that travelers saw. It was once the center of a plantation.

Henry Cogswell Knight, a New England traveler, was struck by seeing abandoned houses in parts of Virginia; the planters had moved on to less exhausted soil.

SCANTLING AND PLANK

(top) The house is an interesting blend of symmetry and asymmetry. Its first section, built circa 1730, has a centrally placed doorway, but it enters directly into the larger of the front rooms. In 1750, one-story wings were added, providing more symmetry and two entry halls on either side of the old front door. However, one wing is deeper than the other.

(bottom) This is a two-story log house with a one-room plan and an odd over-hanging upstairs porch. Its original chimney, much larger, has been replaced.

Southerners and New Englanders disagreed about a lot of things, but by the late 1700s they were in silent agreement on at least one point: They built their houses out of wood.

In 1796 as Isaac Weld rode through Virginia, many of the great plantation houses in the longest-settled areas were built of brick or stone "in the style of the old English manor houses." These he could admire. But "the greater number there, and throughout Virginia, are of wood; amongst which are all those that have been built of later years."

Thomas Jefferson, one of the most revered Virginians, didn't think much of his state's architecture. He loved order, balance, elegance, and permanence, and didn't see much of it in Virginia. He blamed a good bit of this on building in wood. Like Weld, he preferred brick and stone. Yet the homes he saw being built were of "scantling and plank," or boards. He wrote in his *Notes on Virginia* in 1781 that no houses could be uglier or more uncomfortable. The only good thing was that they were also more perishable.

Jefferson thought that his fellow Virginians—and most Southerners, for that matter—built in wood because they believed that brick and stone houses were damp and unhealthy. He carefully refuted this belief, but people were clearly not persuaded. Fifteen years later, Weld heard the same thing when he asked Southerners about their wooden houses. Although this was a widespread conviction, it's probably not the main reason why Virginians and other Southerners built in wood. Just like today, the main reason was probably cost and convenience. The Southern States were heavily forested, so wood was abundant and inexpensive, whereas stone and clay for bricks were harder to find in much of the South.

Jefferson was an architectural absolutist who spent years perfecting Monticello, his own great contribution to domestic architecture. But he was also no democrat when it came to architecture. Not only did he criticize the houses built by his own class—the wealthy planters—he had little

interest in the houses of ordinary people, except to hope that they might somehow, someday, be utterly transformed into buildings that he could approve. Monticello could be admired but not really imitated.

UNEQUAL HOUSING OPPORTUNITIES

The homescape of the South was more remarkably, visibly unequal than anywhere else in the country, including places like New York City and Boston. There were great houses, of course, but many more very small ones. Descriptions from the time, surviving records of the 1798 Direct Tax, and even houses that still stand show that the South had a higher proportion of very small houses than New England or the Middle States.

(above) This story-and-a-half frame house measures 16 ft. by 20 ft. Its gambrel roof provides additional space for the upstairs chamber. The house has one room down, one up, along with a small kitchen in an attached shed.

(right) Built in the early 1800s, this frame house measures 15 ft. by 21 ft. It has a two-room, hall and parlor plan and stairs to the left.

The houses weren't simply smaller in the South, either. The typical Southern house also wasn't as well built or as well maintained as its typical Northern counterpart. Descriptions of travelers line up perfectly: "The manner of building is less substantial than in the Middle or Northern states," Samuel Goodrich wrote in his widely read *Pictorial Geography*. Knight wrote of "shabby farm houses" in 1816. Elias Pym Fordham, traveling the roads of the Chesapeake country in 1817, wrote that "the farm houses, which I have yet seen are mean: the people live in a plain way." John Davis, an Englishman who lived in Virginia and South Carolina from 1820 to 1821, agreed that the houses "are not very superb." He stayed with several different families and wrote that if any one of the houses had "been burnt to the ground, a few boards and a proportionate number of shingles would soon have constructed another."

Other distinctive features of the Southern home caught the traveler's eye. Ceilings were higher. Some great houses had elevated basements, and many more ordinary ones were raised up off the ground on brick or stone piers without a basement at all.

SIMPLY A DIFFERENT WORLD

Small and flimsily built houses may have been typical for many a rural Southerner, but that wasn't necessarily the result of laziness or lack of refinement, as some suggested. The South was, and is, a unique part of the country, with a warmer climate and longer growing season than states north and northwest of Virginia. Also, Southerners lived outdoors as much as indoors. So with the dividing line between indoors and out a bit fuzzy, buttoned-up and weathertight houses weren't as important as in colder places.

Henry Cogswell Knight said most of their houses had their "chimneystacks outside" and that their kitchens were separate buildings, "usually detached a few rods from the house." Chimneys built on the outside of the house took up less space inside. Detached kitchens made houses effectively one room larger. Many houses had "a porch or penthouse, commonly extending the whole length of the building . . . and sometimes all around," Isaac Weld wrote in 1796. In warm weather, porches were living spaces. So were the wide central halls of bigger houses, which usually opened at each end so breezes could blow through. In summertime, people would make their beds in the hall.

Many of these architectural features are what historians call "overdetermined," that is, they can be explained in more than one way. Wide hallways and chimneys at the gable ends of the house were typical in southern England, where many of the people in the South hailed

(top) The one-room house in Dinwiddie County, Virginia was built of thick planks that are dovetail-joined at the corners.

(bottom) This interior view of a small South Carolina log house shows a rough stone fireplace, open stairs going up to the loft, and a small storage space under the stairs.

(top) Dating to the early 1800s; this story-and-a loft log house in Spartanburg, South Carolina has front and rear porches and a substantial stone chimney.

(bottom) Built circa 1830, this is a mix of new and old forms. The main structure is an I house that is one room deep with a central hall and paired internal chimney. It also has a Greek Revival portico and one-story lean-to at rear.

from. But outside chimneys also make sense in a warm climate. A detached kitchen moved the fire out of the living area, which kept the house cooler. And for families that had slaves, detached kitchens also created a social distance between the slaves, who cooked and served, and those who owned and ate. Climate and cultural tradition together helped shape the Southern house.

THE LITTLE HOUSES

"The poorest people build huts of log laid horizontally in pens, stopping the interstices with mud," Jefferson wrote. While there were plenty of rough log houses down South, poor and middling Southerners built more tiny frame houses than log ones. Through 1840, hundreds of thousands of these white families lived crammed into one-room and two-room houses.

Yet, in the idiosyncratic South, even the one-room house existed in distinctive versions. Some were rectangular cabins that probably originated with Scotch-Irish immigrants from Ulster (mostly in the uplands, while squarer, English-descended houses were built farther east). In the very smallest, everything happened in that single room—even cooking. In others, the family cooked in a small shed added to the rear. Frances Kemble Butler described a one-room North Carolina cabin as "a rough brick-and-plank chamber . . . not even whitewashed." Any visitor who was "curious in architecture," she said, would be gratified by the sight of the great beams and rafters that "displayed the skeleton of the building." More spacious one-room houses had lofts and separate kitchens, although these were small and usually windowless.

Davis gives us a glimpse into one of these. It belonged to a family named Strangeways, who had invited him to stay the night while he traveled in Virginia in 1821. The tiny place held only one bed, and Davis wondered where he would sleep. When night fell, his host brought in a ladder from outside, put it against a wall, and "opened a trap-door in the rafters, which I had not perceived." It led to what Davis called "a cock-loft," a small space in the gable of the house, where he was happy to discover a "decent bed."

Two of the most common house types in Virginia and North Carolina (Maryland, too) were based on two-room plans rooted in English tradition. One was the one-story or story-and-a-half "hall and parlor" house, so common from early in the 1600s that it was sometimes called a Virginia house. It had an asymmetrical floor plan, no entry hall, and, frequently, a narrow winder stair up to the loft. Many were no bigger than 16 ft. by 20 ft. Countless Southern families still lived in such places in the 1830s, as their ancestors had nearly 200 years earlier.

(top) A two-story I house from King Williams County, Virginia, with a central doorway dates to the late 1700s or early 1800s. The porch, with its roofed shed section and oddly placed chimney, was added later.

(left) The left section of this house was built in Perquimans County, North Carolina in 1790; the right section around 1825. They were joined to form a center-hallway house.

(top) In Lauderdale County, Alamba, Adam Weaverer built this story-and-a-half log dogtrot or open central passage house in 1838. There are two rooms down and two small bedchambers up—and a space over the passageway.

(right) Amid 1930s canning equipment we can see the fireplace and the rough stairway up to the half-story loft.

The other house type was larger and signaled greater comfort and prosperity. It was the I house—one room deep, two rooms down and two rooms up, with chimneys at both gable ends (a plan view of the house suggested the I shape). In the Middle States, particularly in Pennsylvania, the I house was built of brick or stone and had internal chimneys. In Virginia, it was usually built of wood, with outside chimneys. The earliest versions of the I house were sometimes asymmetrical and usually had two front doors, one for each room. From the mid-1700s on, they were built as Georgian central-hallway houses.

Below North Carolina, travelers found other two-room house types, ones that acquired more striking names. Saddlebag houses were named for a symmetrical shape that reminded people of the balanced leather bags used to carry goods on horseback. These houses had two rooms of equal size, one on either side of a central chimney—something otherwise unusual in most parts of the South. The saddlebag house usually resulted from an addition: The builder took a one-room house with an end chimney and attached another room to that end, with the chimney stuck in the middle.

Dogtrot, sometimes called dog-run, houses had two rooms of the same size connected by an open passage in the center. They were new in the early 1820s, when thousands of families from South Carolina and farther south started building them. James Stuart noticed how common they had become by 1832: "The common form of all the planters' houses is two square pens, with an open space between them, connected by a roof above and a floor below." This breezeway was treated as an additional room, where the family would have dinner or even sleep. The name, which suggests that the family dogs were the real beneficiaries, came later; it does not seem to have been used in the early 1800s.

Although dogtrots were built in both log and frame version, their design responded to the demands of log construction. Because logs were difficult to work with when they became too long, the dogtrot style allowed two separate units to be built and then roofed over, maximizing the "footprint" of the house. They were built in two-story and single-story versions, often with large porches and lean-to additions.

As Stuart saw, dogtrot houses usually weren't built by poor families. They were home to "an ordinary planter, with half a dozen slaves," and could have been at the center of some even more sizable plantations. They reflected the newness of the plantation economy in Georgia, Alabama, and Mississippi and the haste of many planters to clear land and build.

The English traveler Harriet Martineau found an unusually high level of domestic order and cultivation in one planter family's dogtrot

The "plantation village" of Green Hill Plantation, with big house, kitchen, barns, outbuildings, and slave quarters, is perhaps the best-preserved early plantation landscape in the South.

(top) This central-hall I house in Murray County, Georgia, has a two-story porch; its rooms are large but just one deep. Its first owner, James Clement Vann, was a Cherokee chief as well as a prosperous planter.

(bottom) This is one of the Weaver House's upstairs half-story chambers.

In the South, the open breezeway
of a dogtrot house could function as
a room for most of the year as in this
house in Abbeville County, South
Carolina.

house in Alabama, which she described in 1830 as "a log-house, with the
usual open passage in the middle." She could see daylight through the
walls but found an "abundance of books, and handsome furniture."
Although she noted that they were planning to replace it with a larger
frame building, she said that it was a house she "liked exceedingly."

ALMOST LIKE A VILLAGE

From the road or the deck of a steamboat, all the buildings of a plantation
had "the appearance of a village." That's how James Stuart saw things on
an 1832 trip down South. "In front, is the proprietor's house; on either
side, and in the rear, are the hospital, the carriage house, the kitchen, and
the storehouses, and in the rear, a double line of negro houses."

Plantations were laid out just so, in a way that left no doubt who was
in charge or where they lived. The master's "big house," as the slaves
called it, was in front, sometimes reached by a dramatic long drive. Next
came the buildings that served the planter's family and the economy of
the plantation. Farthest in back, usually a few hundred yards away, were
slave cabins.

On the largest plantations the big house could be an extraordinary
structure. Drayton Hall in the countryside near Charleston was an
enduring triumph of Georgian architecture completed in 1742, the home
of several generations of the Drayton family, which was kept up by a
large retinue of household slaves. A monumental 70 ft. by 52 ft., with
two stories and a raised basement for storage and service, Drayton Hall's
stair hall, or "great hall" and "great drawing room," were conspicuous
expressions of wealth and power.

By 1840 some large plantations in Virginia and the Carolinas were
100 to 150 years old, ancient by American standards. These were the
ones, like Drayton Hall, that reminded Isaac Weld of English manor
houses. Many in Alabama and Mississippi were only 10 to 20 years old,
virtually brand new.

*(top) Like Congregationalists, Meth-
odists, and even Catholics in the
1830s, this Baptist congregation built
their church as a Greek temple.*

*(bottom) A great plantation like
Gunston Hall was approached by a
long driveway that offered a series of
impressive views of the surrounding
fields, the grounds, and finally of the
house and outbuildings.*

Virginia Colleges

Founded in 1693, Virginia's College of William and Mary in Williamsburg was Thomas Jefferson's alma mater. He took his degree in 1762 and received an honorary doctorate in 1782. Yet he disliked the college buildings just as much as he did the architecture of Virginia's houses. Most observers admired them, with their steep-hipped roofs, as stately links to the 1690s, but Jefferson called them "rude, misshapen piles, which but that they have roofs, would be taken for brick-kilns." With his designs for the buildings of the University of Virginia, Jefferson advanced his own notions—classical, serene, and balanced—of what the buildings of an educational institution should look like.

Rɪɢʜᴛ: *The faculty and student housing at the University of Virginia was designed by Jefferson in the Roman classical style.* Tᴏᴘ: *Jefferson disliked the architecture of his own college, William and Mary.*

Newer than Drayton Hall by 100 years was Melrose on the Mississippi River in Natchez, with its Greek Revival grandeur and nearly 9,000 sq. ft. of living space. Melrose represented what had come to be the greatest concentration of wealth in the Southern states, the cotton plantations on the extraordinarily rich Mississippi River bottomlands, starting at around New Orleans in the south and running on one, or both, sides of the river up through Tennessee and southern Arkansas. Its two-story kitchen building, with its dimensions of 20 ft. by 40 ft., would have made a very respectable house for most families.

INVESTING IN SLAVERY

Green Hill in Campbell County, Virginia, might well be the best-preserved plantation landscape anywhere in the South. Its cluster of surviving buildings, all dating from the early 1800s, show us what one of Stuart's slaveholding "villages" once looked like on the landscape. Green Hill's "big house" is not a great mansion on the impressive scale of Drayton Hall, although its owner was a wealthy man. It is a solid brick building but plainly built, a central hallway I house with a two-story ell at the rear. Its kitchen and quarters for the domestic slaves are small frame structures.

Green Hill's builder, Samuel Panill, was a highly successful man of business who grew tobacco, ran a grist mill, and owned more than 200 slaves. He trained many of them as carpenters and masons, and they probably played a primary role in building his house. He trained his slaves in order to sell them, as the plantation's surviving auction block suggests. Yet most of the plantation villages were not vast estates surrounding stately mansions. Places like Drayton Hall or Thornhill Plantation in Watsonia, Alambama, with their imposing houses, or models of enterprise like Green Hill dominated the neighborhoods around them and served as the primary symbols of life in the South. Still, they were relatively few in number. No more than 2 to 3 percent of slaveholding families had sufficient resources—100 or more slaves and thousands of acres of land—to match them.

(top) This closeup gives a look at the elaborate portico and doorway of Prospect Hill, begun in 1825 and completed in 1828. The accounts of William Thorne, the owner, show a total expenditure of $2,569.06 for the house, including $1,800 to "Mr. Burgess," the architect/builder, for design and carpentry work.

(bottom) Many slaves were trained as craftsmen on the Green Hill plantation. They stood on this auction block to be sold to those who wanted their skills.

The Great Hall continues to impress visitors to this house, as it has since 1742. The northeast front of the building presented a different face to passers-by on the Ashley River.

(top) Green Hill's log kitchen building is not large as plantation kitchens go, but it has a massive chimney.

(bottom) The interior of the Green Hill kitchen shows a massive double fireplace, possibly indicating that it was used both to cook for the big house and to prepare rations for the slaves in the quarters.

Below Green Hill on the scale of size were thousands of smaller places, with six slaves, or a dozen, or 30. We might today reserve the word "plantation" to mean a great estate, but early observers used the term liberally to describe any agricultural establishment that employed slave labor. John Davis recalled sharing a meal of venison with a South Carolina family in 1821. His host was "a small planter, who cultivated a little rice . . . maintained a wife and four children . . . and owned half a dozen negroes." This plantation consisted of "a solitary log-house in the woods" and a few other log outbuildings.

The worst plantations Frances Kemble Butler ever saw were on the meager, thinly settled lands of the southeast Georgia Pine Barrens in 1838. "Here and there" she found "a few miserable Negro huts squatting around a mean framed building, with brick chimneys built on the outside, the residence of the owner of the land, and his squalid serfs."

A STORY OF TWO HOUSES

One plantation house wasn't necessarily the next. Two British eyewitnesses, Margaret Hunter Hall and Frances Kemble Butler, left us with descriptions of estates in the Deep South. Less than a decade apart, they come across as completely different, yet both women seem to have accurately described what they saw.

Margaret Hall was hard to please and accustomed to finding fault with almost everything she encountered on her family's journey through the United States in 1828–29. But her first visit to a plantation was recorded as an unexpected pleasure. The Halls accepted an invitation to stop at the Skirving Plantation, 50 miles west of Charleston on the Combahee River. The Skirving family had well over 100 slaves, putting them in the upper ranks of plantation owners.

The master and mistress weren't home, but the Halls were welcomed by a crew of household slaves, directed by the "head man," Solomon, who took care of them for the few days they were guests. Before seeing the place, Margaret had "no idea of what a plantation house might be," she wrote to her sister back in England. But, pleased for a change, she found

(above) An interior view shows the archway leading to the stair hall at Mulberry Hill, a Chowan County, North Carolina plantation house.

(left) Cascine in Franklin County, North Carolina, (Southern plant-ers in particular loved to name their houses), built in the 1750s or '60s, has four rooms on the first floor and two rooms above.

HABS NC-6

(top) Many slave houses were small one-room frame stuctures like this row on the Roseberry plantation, not quite in ruins.

(right) This old photograph (taken in the late 1800s) of the Refuge Plantation kitchen in Camden County, Georgia, seems almost to transport us back to the world of slavery. Certainly all of these kitchen utensils could have been found before 1840.

the owner's house "small but very comfortable." The Skirving house had two front parlors—a "dining room and a drawing room"—at least two bedrooms, a wide piazza, and an abundant flower garden.

The absent Mrs. Skirving was apparently a superb housekeeper, and her domestic staff was highly efficient. All was clean and in good order. As the Halls made themselves at home, they discovered all the trappings of domestic comfort—parlor sofa, armchairs, and "snow white quilts and draperies." Visiting the plantation's slave quarters "about five hundred yards from the house," she found 29 two-room cabins and thought them "neatly arranged."

Frances Kemble Butler was an Englishwoman trapped in a failing marriage to Pierce Butler, a planter with an estate on Butler's Island off the Georgia coast. She later claimed that she did not know he was a slaveowner when they married in Philadelphia. Shocked and horrified from her first encounter with slavery, she became the unwilling mistress of a large plantation in 1838.

Like the Skirving Plantation, the Butler estate was large, with at least 200 slaves in its quarters. The Butler house seems to have been about the same size. But the similarities ended there.

"There is little danger of being dazzled by the luxurious splendors of a Southern slave residence," she wrote in a letter to England. As she described it, the Butler house was a story and a half with "three small rooms, and three still smaller, which would be more appropriately designated as closets." The separate kitchen was "a mere wooden out-house, with no floor but the bare earth."

The parlor, "our sitting, eating and living room," was 15 ft. by 16 ft. This was small by the standards of the Philadelphia town houses where she had met her husband, but most American families would have found it large enough. To her, even worse was that the rooms were dingy and crudely finished. Parlor and bedroom were divided by a scuffed wooden partition, not a plastered wall. Upstairs was a single bedchamber under the eaves for her two small children and their nurse. Two of the "closets" were actually the bedroom and office of the plantation's overseer, who shared the house with them.

She found the Butler household slaves willing, but untidy and careless, and difficult for her to instruct. She saw the plantation's slave quarters as squalid and chaotic and struggled unsuccessfully to convince her husband to improve them. Hating to be called "mistress," she discovered neither comfort nor elegance in her house and no satisfaction in her role.

(top) Resplendent in patterned brick, the Episcopal Fork Church in Goochland County, Virginia was built in 1770.

(bottom) St. Peter's Episcopal Church in New Kent County, Virginia, was built in 1700–2; the bell tower to summon worshippers to services was added in 1722. There is a traditional belief that George Washington and Martha Custis were married here in 1756, but, like many stories about Washington, no records have been found to confirm it.

GA., 82-LOUVI, 1-2   HABS   14-2

Built in 1758, this open pavilion was an active marketplace where slaves were bought and sold. Later it became a general market for the town of Louisville, Georgia.

Larger cabins might have a second chimney and two separate "apartments" for families or groups living together. A few had upstairs lofts for sleeping.

On many plantations, one of the cabins also served as the quarters' center for child care. Every morning, children too young to work were taken care of by an elderly woman as their parents labored in the fields.

Like most plantation buildings, slave cabins were built mainly by slaves. In 1822, Peter Neilson came across one being framed on a South Carolina plantation: "I saw one man who was employed in erecting a new hut. He wrought even as late as ten o'clock by the light of a fire, and seemed to handle his saw and plane with considerable dexterity." Slaves generally built and sited them to their master's specifications, not their own. Solomon Northup worked at times as a carpenter while enslaved in Louisiana and was closely supervised.

Isaac Weld in 1796 had observed of Virginia slaves that "many of their small huts are comfortably furnished." Knight thought that the cabins he saw were "cheap and mean, but healthy and comfortable." And the *Pictorial Geography* was anxious to defend the slave houses. All "negro houses have chimneys and two rooms," it contended, adding that American slave cabins were better than the Irish and highland Scottish peasant huts. Not everyone agreed.

Frances Kemble Butler saw two families totaling up to 10 people in each of the 12-ft. by 15-ft. cabins on her husband's plantation. She entered another one "certainly not ten feet square . . . containing three grown-up human beings and eight children . . . which may be called close packing, I think." The Butler Plantation slave cabins provided 10 to 20 sq. ft. per person; the poorest and most crowded houses for free families in Massachusetts, New Jersey, and Maryland provided 40 to 50 sq. ft. But Frances saw slave houses far worse than those on her husband's plantation. After visiting neighboring St. Simons Island, she wrote that "the negro huts on several of the plantations that we passed through were the most miserable human habitations I ever beheld . . . dirty, desolate, dilapidated dog kennels."

Margaret Hall thought that the slave quarters on the Skirving Plantation in South Carolina were "very neatly arranged," but she did notice that few had even a single window; the rest were illuminated only by the open door or a chink between the logs.

Slaves often tended small gardens near their cabins and kept poultry to supplement rations, although sometimes the length of their workday made this impossible.

Despite the enormous difficulties of their lives, slaves were able to maintain embattled but enduring versions of family and community life in the quarters. But the slave cabins themselves were just places to sleep and eat. Neither owned nor rented but assigned, cabins belonged only to the master. Unlike the houses of even the poorest free families, slave cabins weren't independent centers of family life.

THE WORLD OF CHARLESTON

Charleston was the only important American city between Baltimore and New Orleans, and few travelers failed to stop there. It was the capital of a plantation aristocracy, South Carolina's center of power, wealth, and business, with a large community of merchants and long-standing commercial links with northern cities, Liverpool, and London. Growers of rice, indigo, and long-staple sea island cotton often had houses in town in addition to their plantation houses, so Charleston's population swelled in the winter.

(top) Brick slave houses like this one, particularly if they housed only two families, were fairly rare and provided the best living conditions for slave families.

(bottom) A 19th-century engraving illustrates cotton picking on a Southern plantation.

St. Michael's was one of Charleston's
two Episcopal parishes that divided
the city between them. St. Michael's
had a notably tall steeple, which the
traveler Peter Neilson climbed to get
a better view of the city.

*(top) Built in the late 1700s, a
three-and-a-half-story Charleston
townhouse has narrow frontage
(only 26 ft.) and a three-story porch
along its length.*

*(bottom) Charleston's Central
Market building was built in 1841.
It was the center of many commercial activities in the city, including
slave auctions.*

Charleston had almost 30,000 residents in 1840, more than half of them slaves. The city had no need for field hands; they were there to serve their masters and mistresses and to carry on the daily work of the city's wharves and shops.

Visitors delighted in the city's semitropical finery. Climbing to the tall steeple of St. Michael's church in 1822, the Scotsman Peter Neilson saw the city as "a regularly laid out pleasure garden, studded with flower boxes." James Stuart in 1832 found it full of "evergreen shrubs . . . beautiful roses, jonquils, and summer flowers." But its impressive inequalities struck him as well. Other American cities had wide differences between rich and poor, highly unequal distributions of wealth, income, and houses. Yet Charleston seems to have made it especially visible. "There is obviously a great distinction of classes here," concluded Stuart. At the racetrack, he saw that "coaches with coats of arms painted on the doors were not uncommon; and there were several servants in livery."

Some of the houses, Stuart observed, were "worth 10,000£ [or about $30,000 at the time] and [had] real palazzos" with orange trees, magnolias, and palmettos. But in the poorer parts of town, "the houses had a filthy appearance" and the streets were dirty and unpaved.

Time and the hot, humid climate have been kinder to Charleston's brick houses than to its wooden ones and today they represent the bulk of the surviving historic landscape. But observers in the 1820s and 1830s noted that while many large houses were stuccoed brick with slate roofs, most were wooden houses roofed with wooden shingles, like those in the rest of the Southern countryside. In fact, in 1822 Peter Neilson praised the city's newest wooden houses with their "lofty porticoes in front in the Grecian style." He felt that "although the pillars are of timber, being finely painted, they convey an idea of grandeur."

Charleston's most interesting—and most characteristic—houses weren't Greek Revival mansions. In brick or wood, Charleston's builders took two of the typical country styles of architecture—the one-room-deep I house and the two-room-deep central-hall Georgian/Federal house, both two or three stories high—and adapted them for the compactly built city. To fit long, narrow lots, they turned the houses so that

HABS SC-269

(top) Built between 1817 and 1825, the Robinson-Aiken House was one of early Charleston's most opulent residences.

(right) This view of the 1796 Ravenel House shows the open gate of the driveway and the "curtain wall" door that leads into the courtyard.

their gable ends faced the street and enclosed them in courtyards. As Gideon Davis noted in 1830, most of these houses had a piazza or open gallery on every floor, a version of the country porch.

In Charleston, visitors still entered a house through a central doorway on its long side, just as they would have in a typical country house. But to get to that door, they would have had to go through the courtyard gate, which opened from the street. A larger gate opened onto a carriage drive. At the rear of the courtyard, largely invisible from the street, were the "dependencies"—stables, kitchen, and slave quarters, a plantation in miniature. It replaced the vast fields with a courtyard but preserved the architectural separation of masters and slaves.

The largest houses—like the opulent Robinson-Aiken House built in the early 1820s—had three and a half stories, were two rooms deep and two rooms wide on each floor, and had a central hallway. Their slave quarters were the close-packed equivalent of a small village. Smaller houses could be two or two and a half stories and one room deep. These were the houses of Charleston's most successful families, ranging from great plantation owners to prosperous merchants, lawyers, and physicians.

Most of the city's slaves lived in the quarters behind their owners' imposing houses. Yet Charleston also had artisans, clerks, and shopkeepers and their families, white and free black alike. The houses of these city's more ordinary families have lost out over the years to fires, hurricanes, neglect, and the selective pressures of urban development. The Gibbes House, probably built around 1835, is a surviving example of more commonplace houses. The two-story frame I house is one room deep, 19 ft. wide, and a sort of smaller, narrower version of the more impressive houses of the well-to-do, with its two piazzas and central-hallway entrance away from the street.

A brick house on Chalmers Street, built sometime before 1780, is a much smaller city house. It has two and a half stories, with one room on each floor and a kitchen at the rear. It's the kind of house that Neilson or Palmer would have ignored altogether. Tradition says that this house was once a tavern and, if so, it would have been a very crowded one.

Peter Neilson stayed in Charleston for more than a year, long enough to witness two of the greatest threats to the city, fire and storm. Over the course of his stay he saw several big fires. Because "the greater part of the houses in Charleston" were made of wood, he began, "fires are consequently very destructive." The occasional fire also helps explain the selective survival of Charleston's brick buildings. During one fire, Neilson witnessed houses on the opposite side of the street bursting into flames from the intense heat.

(top) The Crane House is a smaller two-and-a-half-story version of the characteristic Charleston courtyard house.

(bottom) An interior view of this dependency or outbuilding of the Hayward House shows the kitchen fireplace and oven. The stairway leads to the slave quarters above.

This two-and-a-half-story house with one room on each floor and a kitchen at the rear gives us a sense of the housing of Charlestonians who were not planters (or slaves).

The Stuart House is a frame three-and-a-half-story townhouse built around 1800. Its front door opens onto an inside stair hall, not a courtyard.

Given that their houses were so closely packed together, Charlestonians commonly resorted to desperate measures to protect their homes and their city. When the flames seemed impossible to stop, they dragged out barrels of gunpowder and proceeded "to blow up two or three houses" in the path of the blaze, depriving the fire of fuel. This had its own risks. "Accidents frequently occur from these explosions, as the crowd have generally very little time to retire to a suitable distance."

On September 27, 1822, a powerful hurricane struck the city. It came with no warning, as all storms did until relatively late in the 20th century. For several hours that night, Neilson and his American hosts huddled in the safest place they could find and listened to "the crashing of houses and chimneys and the rattling of tiles, bricks and timber." The next morning, he surveyed the damage. Most houses had lost their shutters and windowpanes,

---

Few Schools and Far Between

In the South, wrote Harriet Martineau, "sons take land and buy slaves very early, so that education is less thought of, and sooner ended, than in almost any part of the world." Schools are few and far between in the HABS collection for the Southern States, which expresses something important about the region. Formal schooling simply wasn't terribly important in the early South. Prosperous planters ensured the education of their children, but nearly one white adult in five was illiterate. Of course, few slaves could read

With its bell frame this probably was a school building on the Mansfield Plantation in Georgetown County, South Carolina.

and, in some states, it was illegal to teach them.

Compared with the Middle States or New England, the South was a far more spoken culture, a place of storytelling, long memories, and even unwritten account keeping. Some schools and academies were privately supported schools, but they had limited reach. Scattered settlement and long distances made access to any school difficult. Some wealthy families had resident tutors, or they opened schools on the plantation for white children in the neighborhood.

The east and west sides of a Charleston brick double house built circa 1770 are mirror images.

"carried in like sheets of paper." The storm also carried the several-ton bell tower of a church several hundred feet away from its mooring. Again, Charleston's wooden houses suffered the greatest damage. Many were completely "overturned with their contents."

And Charleston was not a healthy place. Every June the South Carolina lowlands faced yellow fever. Families that could, left the swampy coast for the city itself. Some who could afford to travel farther left the city for the safer climate of New England (life expectancies for rural Massachusetts were considerably better than for Charleston). Others went to the uplands of the Carolina Piedmont, where they stayed until October or November. But most of Charleston's people had little choice but to stay. "There have been instances of families," Isaac Holmes reported, "consisting of a father, mother and four or five children, whom the yawning grave has received at one time."

During his year in the city, Peter Neilson tracked the impact of the disease. Because of the heat, people had to be buried quickly, so carpenters kept "a large assortment of different sized coffins ready made." He also saw shop windows full of coffin plates ready to be engraved with the name of the deceased, which was not "an agreeable sight for a stranger in times of sickness."

Neilson attended services in several Charleston churches. In each, the pews were unusually wide to fend off heat. Because families owned their own pews, most churches had a separate gallery for strangers and one on "the other side for colored people." It appears that Charleston kept the Sabbath far better than New Orleans. Neilson witnessed vast crowds taking communion at the Presbyterian church. The first service involved nearly 300 white women—and three men. At a later service the same day, he saw "several hundred blackpeople of both sexes."

NEW ORLEANS:
LIKE ANOTHER COUNTRY

In the early 1800s, travelers got to New Orleans a number of different ways. Most people who left descriptions came from the east, usually by stagecoach or private carriage from Mobile, Alabama. But people ceaselessly moved in and out of the city by water as well, disembarking at the harbor after a strenuous ocean voyage, poling down the Mississippi on a flatboat, or coming down on a steamboat.

They were surprised by New Orleans but usually not enchanted. The cultural texture of the South had local variations, but it was overwhelmingly English, Scotch-Irish, and African-American. Particularly for those who had just passed through this rural South, the cultural complexity of New Orleans was a shock.

There were more than 100,000 people in New Orleans by 1840, making it the fourth-largest city in the United States, behind New York, Philadelphia, and Baltimore and ahead of Boston and Charleston. With its French and Spanish colonial history, its population was even more assorted than New York's. And its semitropical luxuriance made it far more exotic.

"New-Orleans appears less American, than any city I have visited," Henry Cogswell Knight wrote in 1819. "It reminded me of prints of French and Spanish cities." James Stuart, visiting in 1832, found that in New Orleans "inhabitants from every state in the union and from every country in Europe, mixed with the Creoles, and all the shades of the coloured population, form an astonishing contrasts of manners, languages and complexions."

(top) The "old brick church" of 1788 overlooks its crowded graveyard, with many aboveground tombs.

(bottom) When slaves came to church with their owners in St. Andrew's, they sat apart in this high gallery. Virtually all American churches, north and south, had segregated seating.

(top) The Cabildo, the Spanish seat of government for New Orleans was built in 1794; after the Louisiana Purchase in 1803, it became the New Orleans city hall until 1831.

(bottom) The Beauregard House, a wide-spreading 1826 Greek Revival house, with nine rooms, has one full story and a raised basement. The separate kitchen and slave quarters are to the rear of the courtyard.

Roughly 24,000 of the city's people were slaves, and the New Orleans Exchange, with its almost daily auctions, was the nation's largest slave market. Like today, people in New Orleans do things their own way. For instance, the law allowed masters and mistresses to send their slaves to the city jail, where the sheriff would whip them. James Stuart, coming in late one night, found that the household slaves "had no beds, however, to sleep upon—all lying, like dogs, in the passages of the house."

It was a multilingual city, where French could be heard in the streets as often as English. Stuart saw street signs in French and complained that "very many of the storekeepers are unable to speak English."

The true language of the city, however, was money. Its enormous economic vitality was evident to all. Nature had collaborated with the city's ambitions by funneling all trade along the great Mississippi Valley through a single place. Visitors counted the barges and steamboats coming down the river, "the forests of masts all around" (as Margaret Hall said) of ships ready to sail for Northern cities and ports in Europe, and the thousands of bales of cotton and bushels of wheat on the wharves. By the early 1830s, Stuart could number "1500 flat boats lying at the sides of the levee at a time," as well as 50 steamboats loading and unloading. Along with the boats came "5000 or 6000 boatmen."

The city was also famed for moral disorder, at least by American Protestant standards. Gambling parlors and billiard halls were open day and night. It was well known for its brothels, although the "fallen women" looked and dressed so respectably that travelers could not distinguish them on the street.

The people of New Orleans took Sunday in the Catholic, continental fashion as a day of rest and recreation, not of strict religious observance. Although the rule for the country as a whole was for businesses to close on Sunday, in New Orleans, stores were open. In 1819, Fortescue Cumings thought that Sunday was the busiest shopping day of the week. Walking on the levee, he saw the city's slaves taking a holiday. There were "vast numbers of negro slaves, men, women, and children, assembled together on the levee, drumming, fifing, and dancing, in large rings." Many enjoyed all this, although the New Orleans Sabbath shocked others, particularly straitlaced Scotsmen and New Englanders accustomed to the ways of Edinburgh and Boston.

Although travelers enjoyed describing the women of New Orleans, who often wore light caps or veils instead of American bonnets, it was a city of unmarried men. Censuses show that New Orleans had far more young men in proportion to women than any other American city—an

imbalance that helps explain its reputation as a place of easy virtue.

EARTH TOO WET FOR THE DEAD

New Orleans geography had always been perilous, protected from the mighty river that threatened its low-lying existence by a levee of packed earth. By 1805 the levee already extended "from fifteen miles below the city to fifty miles above it, forming a good road all the way," Thaddeus Mason Harris wrote. Many travelers observed that people spoke of going "up" to the river, rather than "down." The water, after all, was considerably higher than the town and ships' masts would tower over the streets. They also noticed that the inhabitants were always watching the levee, keeping "a sharp look out for crevasses," as Margaret Hall said.

(top) The three-window-wide façade to the left is the Gally House, a large three-story brick townhouse built in 1830.

(right) This piece of French colonial architecture, prominent in the city center, was one of the buildings that made the city seem unlike other American places. It was built in 1727–34 as the convent for the Ursuline nuns, who teach in New Orleans to the present day. It remained a convent until 1824. In 1831 it was briefly the state capitol, then in 1834 it became the residence of the Archbishop of New Orleans.

When the David Olivier House, a circa 1820 plantation house, was built, it was well on the outskirts of New Orleans. There is a two-story gallery all around the house.

Given the swampy ground, builders rarely tried to dig cellars in New Orleans. When they did try, the excavations had "uniformly fallen in and filled with water," Harris was told. And not surprisingly, no one had much good to say about the city's streets, which naturally suffered from the condition of the soil and the high water table. Charles Daubney in 1838 found them unpaved and "almost impassable for mud."

There were more imminent perils as well. The city was also a dangerously unhealthy place, visited throughout the year by malaria and yellow fever. As we know now, the ever-present mosquitoes brought both. Although James Stuart saw mosquito netting over the beds in the city's hotels, they were there purely for comfort while sleeping. Mosquitoes swarmed everywhere, breeding in swampy pools, open water barrels, and mud puddles on the streets.

In the summer, the yellow fever "appears simultaneously in various quarters of the city, through which it stalks like a destroying angel," Martineau wrote. The toll was highest on newcomers, since longtime residents had survived previous attacks and acquired some immunity. Of those strangers attacked, Martineau was told, "not above two-thirds survive."

The public burying ground was a stretch of swampy ground about a half mile from the city center. Every day its keepers had to ensure that 20 to 30 graves of different sizes were opened, which were often filled before nightfall. Gravediggers experienced great difficulty sinking the coffins into the wet ground, so coffins usually had holes bored in them so they would fill with water in what was called "the wet grave." New Orleans' wealthier families bought plots in graveyards closer in and were interred in brick and plaster tombs aboveground. They preferred to be kept above the water level.

LAND OF HEAT AND FEVER

New Orleans was likely the most dangerous place to live in the United States. To more than a few observers, these painful circumstances meant that the city was entirely about gain and greed because nothing else could explain why men would risk their lives and those of their families in "so ill-favoured, so pestilential a city, this city of cotton and yellow fever," as the Englishman Charles Daubney called it in 1838.

Despite its well-known perils and the shadows of slavery, the cityscape attracted and fascinated visitors. Unlike other American cities, New Orleans centered around the religious and governmental buildings of the old French and Spanish regime—the Cathedral of St. Louis, the Cabildo or administrative center, and the convent of the Ursuline nuns. "The church, town-house, jail, convent, bank, theatre, and governor's palace," thought Harris, "would, in any country, be esteemed large and handsome buildings." Looking beyond the square, he saw that "most of the houses have open galleries, and gardens abounding with flowering shrubs and rich bearing orange-trees. These give the city a cool and lively appearance, and convey to my mind very pleasurable sensations."

Travelers saw an architecture adapted to the climate and terrain, with a French Caribbean or Mediterranean air. Houses had open galleries, what Henry Cogswell Knight called "airy piazzas," and were "elevated on piles, with cellars above ground" (which we call crawlspaces today). Fortescue Cumings observed in 1808 that "the rooms are lofty, and the doors very wide, to admit a free circulation of air, which in this warm climate is very necessary." Roofs were not shingled but covered with flat French tiles. Doors were often left open during the day and screened with long white muslin curtains. In contrast, Harriet Martineau singled out one city house that had been built by a transplanted Englishman.

These shotgun houses on a planta-tion give a sense of this distinctive house form that was emerging in Louisiana in the 1830s and '40s.

(top) Catherine Duduan, a "free woman of color," bought this property in 1807 and had a four-room stuccoed brick house built. Its pentagonal shape reflects the jog in the street. It was painted yellow and roofed with red tile.

(bottom) Visible is one of three buildings on a narrow plot, a one-story, four-room house built in 1811. Behind it is a second and smaller two-story structure, two rooms up and two down. Deeper in this narrow lot is a third house, a one-story, two-room building.

It was, she said, "obstinately inappropriate to the scene and climate; red brick, without gallery, or even eaves and porch; the mere sight of it was scorching."

The remarkable old buildings that make New Orleans so distinctive today are a partial survival of the houses of the early city. As in Charleston, what survives of the oldest are brick and stuccoed and for the same reasons—fire and storm. Up through the 1830s, "the houses in front of the town" were brick but elsewhere were mostly of wood. Ordinary city houses were "generally of one story, and the principal apartment opens at once on the street," the Scotsman Thomas Hamilton wrote in 1832.

Some of these houses survived to be photographed. One is the LaRionda Cottage, on Burgundy Street, built in 1811. It is a one-story house of stuccoed brick, 29 ft. by 40 ft., with four rooms and a small detached kitchen. Both front doors open directly onto the street. Another, about half its size, is a small framed house, on Chartres Street, of one story and a loft. It has two rooms and a kitchen shed. Houses like these are where most of the city's free population of artisans and shopkeepers and their families, both white and black, lived.

AT HOME IN THE CITY

The most interesting houses in New Orleans were the ones that still grab us today, the big townhouses of old plantation families, well-off merchants, steamboat-line operators, cotton brokers, and others who prospered in the boom years. These were the "edifices of greater pretension," as Hamilton called them, "covered with stucco, and adorned with verandas." In their various colors—white, rose, or yellow—he enjoyed them for providing "pleasing variety" to the eye. He also noted a part of the city where "Anglo-American" Greek Revival houses were rapidly going up. But he dismissed them as inappropriate to the landscape, as "larger, but bare and unseemly."

The C. H. Taney House, built in 1807–8, is a good example of an early house "of greater pretension" but relatively modest size. It had two stories and an attic, although the first floor, in characteristic New Orleans fashion, was built to be used as a store. Upstairs, according to an 1834 description, were "four large rooms . . . a rear gallery and a front balcony" with a separate kitchen building (and slave quarters) in the rear. The attic was low and undoubtedly very warm. Visitors entered such houses by going through the porte cochere, or passageway into the brick-paved courtyard, and up a flight of steps to the second-floor entrance.

A far grander example designed along the same lines is the Girod House, built circa 1810. At three and a half stories and with imposing

dimensions of 62 ft. by 105 ft., it provided abundant living space of 12 or more rooms, even with its first floor given over to commercial use. An attached dependency provided quarters for several slaves. An equally large and elegant building, but built with different intentions, is the Gally House, built in 1830. On its small lot, the street floor was devoted to commerce, but its upper floors were divided into three two-and-a-half-story apartments, each with five rooms, a separate staircase, balcony, and rear gallery. These arrangements assumed that the tenants would be reasonably prosperous slave-owning families. At

(above) A good example of an early New Orleans house of modest size but greater striving for style is the C. H. Taney House, built in 1807–8.

(right) Built in 1796 as a parish house for the Catholic mission in then Spanish-ruled Natchez, Missippippi, this striking house has a brick first story with cypress siding above.

Built in 1845, Melrose is a powerful expression of the enormous wealth accumulated by planters on the fertile lands of the lower South. The main plantation house in Natchez, Missippippi, has over 9,000 sq. ft. of living space.

the rear of the small courtyard is a large building with three sets of kitchens and slave quarters.

Margaret Hall, who despised American frame houses, was a guest in a New Orleans townhouse for a few weeks in 1828. She announced that she far preferred them to the "pitiful wood things universal elsewhere, for which I have not yet got over my contempt." She particularly liked their courtyards, gated passageways, and porches, which looked "deliciously cool for summer use."

Despite its well-known dangers, New Orleans continued, in its own complicated way, to flourish. It was an exotic city full of sights, sounds, great food, and unique architecture that could be experienced nowhere else in America. It was also an American boom town, full of adventurous young men set on making their fortune in commerce. As J. E. Alexander wrote in 1832, it was *sui generis*, a unique American place.

Going Upriver to the West

A traveler on a steamboat heading up the great river from New Orleans had several days and more than 100 miles to observe the riverfront plantations that were the greatest wealth of the Southern States.

In 1833, Thomas Hamilton found the landscape monotonous, preferring the wild scenery of the Mississippi's upper stretches. For him, there was "nothing to be seen except plantations of sugar, cotton and rice, with the houses of their owners, and the little adjoining hamlets inhabited by the slaves."

But William Loughton Smith found the sight extraordinary. "The country is wonderfully fine," he wrote in 1824. "No description of mine can do justice to the appearance of its principal establishments." He saw vast fields "under the highest state of cultivation." He observed slave quarters with 40 to 50 cabins. He passed sugar mills and cotton presses and large warehouses for storing "the immense productions of the plantations." Beyond these working areas were "the most superb houses . . . second to none in size, architecture, or decorations." And "towards evening, the piazzas and porticos of the houses are filled with ladies."

One other memorable sight marked the transition northward into the Western States. On the east bank of the river were two settlements called Natchez. Overlooking the river and a steep climb up the bank was Natchez on the Hill, a respectable town of merchants and planters.

Far below it was Natchez under the Hill, the landing where planters brought their cotton to be shipped to New Orleans and where river boatmen came for trade and recreation. It was also known as one of the wildest places in the early United States. The taverns never closed, prostitution and gambling were constantly available, and the streets were full of fights. Since tavern doors were open to the street, wrote Smith, he could see that they were "full of men and women of the most abandoned habits, dancing, drinking, and uttering the most obscene language." The steamboat's crew advised him to stay close to the wharf, "for the risk of being robbed was considerable."

These were the contrasting images of the Southern States that travelers would take with them as they went upriver. They would remember the great plantation—a world of admirable elegance for a few, sustained by the labor of many. They would also remember the wild and profligate world of the boatmen, who brought the great plantations' crops to market. Neither reflected the lives of most Southerners, but they captured something vital. The American South was a land of great extremes.

The stair hall of the Auburn Plantation in Natchez boasts a remarkable spiral staircase.

THE WEST

A COUNTRY OF MOVERS

The American West was the future of America and on that point everybody agreed. But, like the future, the West was immense and barely understood. So the Southerners and Easterners and foreigners who traveled to the West came to see a new country in the making, sometimes to better understand what the country's future looked like, but more often to be a successful part of that future.

Every year great streams of emigrants headed west. Southerners came up the Mississippi from New Orleans or struggled west through the mountain gaps from Virginia and the Carolinas. From Pennsylvania, New Jersey, and Maryland, they traveled on the great roads through the Alleghenies to Pittsburgh or Wheeling and then on to Cincinnati by water. From New England and New York, they took the roads west out of Albany. After 1825, the Erie Canal and steamboats on Lake Erie made this northern route the least difficult way to the West.

The people of the Western States were "the descendants or natives of almost every European country and every Atlantic State," Goodrich's *Pictorial Geography* said. The routes roughly followed lines of latitude, so western New York and northern Ohio are sometimes called "New England extended." From there, people went on to northern Indiana, Illinois, and Michigan. And the most adventuresome just kept going.

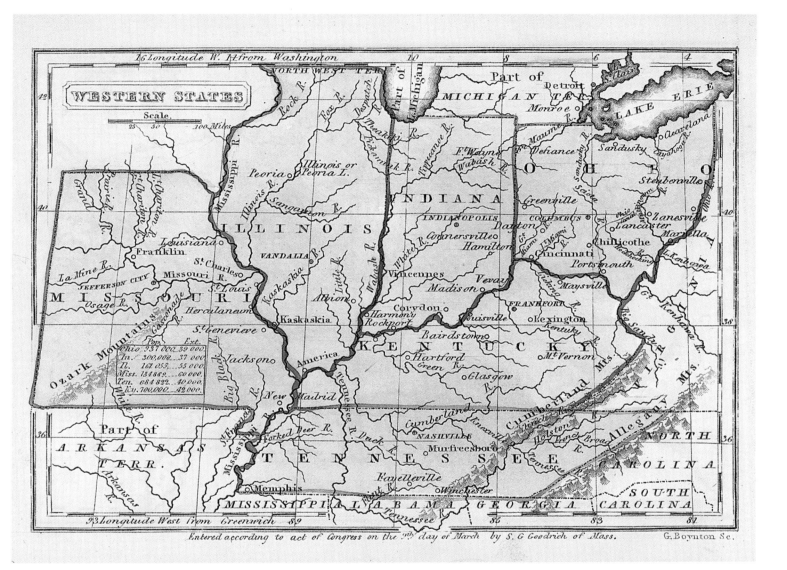

(top) *A dogtrot log house in Racola, Missouri, was clapboarded over at some point between the late 1790s when it was built and 1936 when this photograph was shot. The dogtrot has been enclosed, to give it a single front door and hallway.*

(right) *This wider view of the Peter Burr House shows it in its farm setting with later outbuildings.*

This engraving, titled "The Beginning," provides an idealized version of a pioneer family in the 1830s.

Virginians and Carolinians first settled Kentucky, and some went on to Tennessee and Arkansas. But wherever you went from Ohio to Missouri were settlers from the Middle States. And in many of these freshly hewn frontier states and territories, the unique qualities that made somebody *from* one part of the country or another began to merge and blur.

WEST ON THE PENNSYLVANIA ROAD

In September 1819, James Flint traveled from Philadelphia to Pittsburgh by stagecoach, about 300 long and jarring miles (to better understand what riding in one of these was like, try taking a very slow ride down a rutted dirt road in the back of an old pickup truck). The coach, which also carried the U.S. Mail, took the central Pennsylvania route over the Allegheny Mountains. All along Flint's way the road was thronged with "movers." This huge

---

❋ EVERYDAY LIFE ❋

A Roadside Village

Travelers passing through Wayne County, Indiana on the National Road in 1840 could have stopped at the newly built Mansion House Tavern in Centerville. The village, in fact, had grown up around the road in the early 1830s. When its width was changed from 100 feet to 65 feet, some enterprising residents built additions to their houses and shops that brought them closer to the road—and to customers. The Lantz House in Centerville is connected by an

LEFT: An arch connects this brick house and a carriage-making shop on the old National Road in Centerville, Indiana. The house was built between 1831 and 1836. RIGHT: The public rooms were on the first floor of this circa 1840 tavern in Centerville, Indiana, which was built to serve traffic on the National Road. Bedchambers were in the upper floors.

archway to its Carriage Shop, which was built to be nearer to roadside traffic. Such towns and villages thrived along the National Road, which for several decades served as the great path of westward migration, bringing hundreds of settlers past the Mansion House Tavern and other commercial spots along the road each month. The road was eclipsed by the railroads later in the century and saw a revival of traffic only with the advent of the automobile age.

EMIGRATING FROM CONNECTICUT TO EASTERN OHIO IN 1805, DISTANCE 608 MILES, TIME 30 DAYS, NUMBER OF PASSENGERS 10.

(top) Othniel Looker, a farmer and schoolteacher, came from New Jersey to Hamilton County near Cincinnati and built this brick house in 1804. It has two first-floor rooms and two bedchambers under the eaves with dormer windows.

(bottom) Entitled "Emigrants from Connecticut," this engraving depicts the overland west for a fairly prosperous family. The covered wagon, which had canvas stretched over wooden arches, would have required a fairly substantial investment. Inside, the mother holds her baby as the father prods the team and the milk cow follows behind.

annual migration peaked every September, just before traveling weather gave out, but also because farmers had to wait until then to harvest and sell their crops.

Because the stagecoach traveled faster than the movers, Flint passed hundreds of them and got a good look at them and the things they were hauling into the new land. As he described them, the emigrants were as varied as the pilgrims in Chaucer's *Canterbury Tales*—Irish and Germans and people from every one of the Middle States.

The best equipped made the way in large horse-drawn wagons, "the young and the strong walking, the aged and infants riding." They passed a new kind of vehicle, lumbering and slow, something Flint had never seen before: wagons covered with canvas "stretched over hoops that pass from one side of the waggon to the other, in the form of an arch . . . the front is left open, to give the passengers within the vehicle the benefit of a free circulation of cool air."

Those who traveled light, or who just didn't own much, had smaller, one-horse carts. The poorest walked. At one particularly tough spot through the mountains, Sidelong Hill, Flint met "a singular party of travelers—a man with his wife and ten children." All 12 were walking. The oldest son had the youngest child "tied on his back" and the father was pushing a wheelbarrow that contained all their possessions. They told Flint that they had come from New Jersey and were headed for Ohio. From Pittsburgh they would take a riverboat the rest of the way.

After he got to Pittsburgh, Flint continued his emigrant watching. Covered wagons sometimes rumbled through in trains of three or more, carrying big extended families or groups of neighbors. Movers also came in coaches and on horseback.

Most of them went on to start farms in western Pennsylvania, Ohio, or even farther west, but some stayed in Pittsburgh, a town that was just then, in the early 1800s, growing into a city (in 1790 it had fewer than 2,000 people but by 1840 it was a city of more than 21,000). Sited where the Allegheny and Monongahela rivers form the Ohio, it became a center of commerce, transportation, and manufacturing, with ironworks,

(top) The Nixon tavern, on the Fairchance Road in Fairchance, Pennsylvania, was probably built around 1810. It is a log house with one-story and two-story sections.

(right) Located in Racola, Missouri, this structure consists of two log houses joined at one corner, one with an overhanging roof that forms a porch. Both houses are roofed with hand-split shake shingles.

glassworks, and foundries. To the Frenchman Andre Michaux, Pittsburgh was spectacularly situated. In 1802 it presented "the most pleasing view, produced by the perspective of the rivers." The Ohio flowed majestically west away from the city, "and to appearance, loses itself in space." Michaux also thought that Pittsburgh's hillside setting made it especially healthy, thanks to its "very salubrious" air.

A few years later, Fortescue Cuming also admired the town's "fine situation" but found that, by then, Pittsburgh's bituminous coal, "as fine . . . as any in the world," was transforming the landscape. Coal was so abundant, so close, and so easily dug out of the hills that every house in the community heated and cooked with it. The result was that Pittsburgh's lovely views were dimmed by coal soot as early as 1809.

The exteriors of its houses, however well built, had a "dirty and disagreeable appearance" to Cuming. In 1841 Charles Dickens described it as a city that "certainly has a great quantity of smoke hanging about it" but later noted that, as an Englishman accustomed to the coal fires of London, he could not in fairness complain.

OLD WAYS AND NEW

The West was new, but to a lot of Americans who were headed that way it signified a return to the past, to more land, more freedom, more opportunity than they had in the settled parts of the East Coast. Americans in New England and the Middle States were already having fewer children by 1800. But new settlers still reared the larger families of pre-Revolutionary times, responding in part at least to greater opportunity on the land.

Moving was a wager on the future. It set unrelenting work, hardship, privation, and danger against the hope of independence and future prosperity. Charles Daubney realized this in 1838 when he visited a sizable farm in Arkansas that had a tiny and uncomfortable log house. The farmer was far from poor, "yet he contented himself with a log hut, such as none but common laborers would be contented to occupy in Europe," the Englishman wrote. Standards of living out on the frontier were necessarily lower, even for people with the means to do better—at least for the first generation. It was almost always a long way to town. Besides, they had work to do, land to clear, and crops to plant and harvest.

In some new settlements, with houses only half built, people were for a time more crowded than they would be in the cities, James Flint wrote. He passed through places where he saw "several families frequently

The John Karns House is a handsome and rare example of an early Pittsburgh townhouse.

Named for its hilltop setting, Cragfont in Sumner County, Tennessee, is a large stone central-hallway house that was visited by the Frenchman Andre Michaux just after it was completed by General James Winchester in 1802. Michaux admired the view and called the house "very elegant for the country."

(top) This remarkable picture captures a childhood moment outside a country school in Sevier County, Tennessee, from 1936. The 19th-century school building is constructed of sawn planks, not logs, and dovetailed at the corners.

(bottom) The deep front overhang that creates a porch on this one-and-a-half-story log house never had posts supporting it. Instead, it is supported by logs that are cantilevered from the side walls. The small house probably has only one room down and one up. A small frame shed addition is visible at the rear.

inhabiting a house of one apartment, without any inner door, so that when the street door is open, passengers may see the inmates at table." Temporary accommodations could be truly desperate. Flint saw "families living in temporary huts built of small pieces of decayed timber collected in the woods." Once he saw a family living "for several weeks, under an old waggon that was turned upside down."

For most people, the journey west—the journey to an earlier time—meant either primitive discomfort, uncorrupted freedom, or both. Anne Royall remembered fondly the log houses where she grew up in western Pennsylvania when she toured the western country of Kentucky and Illinois and saw the log cabins there. Zerah Hawley, a doctor who came to northeastern Ohio from Connecticut, saw the privations of the frontier as a sort of return to the Dark Ages, an abandonment of civilization.

The most optimistic version of the story of the West entailed continuous improvement and progress. As Timothy Flint described Kentucky, a settler family would arrive "in the midst of the primeval scene" and start to clear the forest. Soon they would have "a comfortable cabin, and other outbuildings." Two years later, there would be "extensive fields and abundant orchards."

In 10 years, the log buildings would be gone and the family would be living in a fine new house of frame or brick. The landscape would be one of settled farms and small towns. Gristmills and sawmills would be running and the great forest would be a fading memory.

SOMETIMES THE ROAD LED TO DEFEAT

In chronicling the success of New England emigrants out West, John Abbott wrote that this progression was "the history of tens of thousands." Although many did succeed, many others found the progress a much slower process than they'd imagined. The log house never became truly comfortable, and the fields took many years to clear completely. In 1838, Andrew Bell saw log houses in the Western States that were "the same temporary or make-shift building which the settler put up ten or twenty years ago, when he first came into the forest."

More than a few had their hopes crushed. Emigrating was really only for the young and vigorous, wrote Horace Greeley, the famed editor of the *New York Tribune,* recalling his family's experience with pioneering. Greeley was a 15-year-old printer's apprentice who stayed in Vermont when his parents decided to leave in 1826 for western Pennsylvania's Erie County. Ezekiel Greeley was 41 and Mary Greeley was 38. Their son thought they "had plunged into the primitive forest too late in life."

Over 30 years, the progress was painfully slow. The Greeleys built three log houses, each one a bit better than the next. Greeley's father was fairly happy with the situation, but his mother never really warmed to the West: "The chimney of the best log house," she insisted, "would smoke, and its roof, in a driving rain, would leak, do what you might."

In the early 1800s, most roads in the Western States were as rough as this one, although travelers passing by this log house in Ohio would have seen tree stumps and newly cleared land, not this underbrush.

(top) The two-story stone section of
the Croghan House in Pittsburgh
was built around 1825; the massive
three-story addition with columned
piazzas was built in the 1840s.

(right) Mowry Brown, a carpenter
who was born in Rhode Island and
emigrated to Illinois in his early 20s,
built this Greek Revival side-hall
house in the early 1840s near
Rockford.

By the time they were in their 60s, they finally had a frame house, but it was small and poor. His mother was disappointed and worn out from hard work and discomfort. Greeley wrote of his mother: "I never caught the old smile on her face from the day she entered those woods until that of her death."

AMERICAN IMPROVEMENTS

Princeton, Indiana, was so new in 1818 that the tree stumps hadn't yet rotted away in the streets, which made it "dangerous to walk in after dark," Elias Pym Fordham wrote. In 1807, there had been only one small cabin there. Just two years after Indiana's statehood in 1816, there were "three small brick, four or five frame, and seven or eight log, houses, and about a dozen cabins," he wrote.

There were a few great mansions scattered throughout the vast expanse of the Western States as well as many good-size houses, but, on average, Western houses were the smallest by far in the country. The West stood for the architecture of improvisation. As late as 1838, the Scotsman Andrew Bell was struck by how many still had "no more than one room, which is both kitchen and sitting room, cellar and dormitory."

Some families in the West went from log houses to brick or stone houses but most didn't. The census of 1840 reported that, of new houses built during the previous year in the West, about 90 percent were made of wood. Ohio had the most brick and stone architecture—one house in four. This reflected not only the state's growth but also the persistent influence of Pennsylvania. Traditional New England, Pennsylvania, and Southern house types were seen in the West; some houses showed bits of several influences. The farther west you went, the more these clear-cut types merged and blurred and the harder it was to pick out the origins.

In places along the Mississippi River in Indiana, Illinois, and Missouri, some surviving buildings echoed an earlier history of French settlement. Dickens noted some of them in St. Louis in 1841, as "built of wood, with tumble-down galleries before the windows." With their "high garret gable-windows peeking into the roofs," he thought that they had "a kind of French shrug about them . . . as if they were grimacing in astonishment at the American Improvements." Those improvements were the new houses going up to replace the old Creole buildings.

There wasn't much good architecture in the West and so not much to see, opined the *Pictorial Geography*. Although this wasn't completely true,

Built in 1841, this was one of the new houses that were going up in St. Louis at the time of Charles Dickens' visit. It's an I house with two and a half stories above a raised basement.

The public rooms were on the first floor of this circa 1840 tavern in Centerville, Indiana, which was built to serve traffic on the National Road. Bedchambers were in the upper floors.

HABS NO. IN-104-1

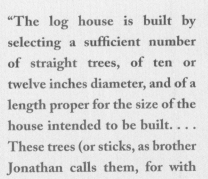

Peter Allen, a physician from Connecticut, built this stately and elegant side-hall Greek Revival house sometime around 1830 near Kinsman in eastern Ohio.

This one-room log structure, which is only 26 ft. by 20 ft., was built in the 1770s in Fayette County, southwestern Pennsylvania.

most observers put their descriptive energies into depicting the world of the log house, the preeminent symbol of frontier settlement. Travelers were sometimes pleasantly surprised by fancier brick and frame houses but often found that even these shared in the temporary and provisional quality of life in the Western States.

In 1819, Henry Cogswell Knight spoke like a true New Englander, somebody used to the amenities of hallways and vestibules. The greatest fault he found with houses in the West was "the out-doors opening directly into the parlours, so that in winter they are quite comfortless."

Andrew Bell gave credit to Western "houses which are owned by industrious, and managing men." These had "a peculiarly neat, and some of them elegant appearance," he wrote in 1838. However, he didn't find many of them. Many houses that might otherwise be impressive and imposing were unkempt or unfinished, inside and out. Broken windows were

---

⊛ EVERYDAY LIFE ⊛

How to Build a Log House

"The log house is built by selecting a sufficient number of straight trees, of ten or twelve inches diameter, and of a length proper for the size of the house intended to be built. . . . These trees (or sticks, as brother Jonathan calls them, for with him, every tree, however large, is a stick) are laid one upon another, without any preparation but taking off all the branches, and notching the ends, so as to form a sort of dovetail at the angles. . . . A door-place, and window places are cut out, where wanted, with a saw, and the frames being put in, hold the ends of the timbers in their proper places.

"The entire wall is then generally, but not always, hewn with a broad axe, to something like a smooth face, the crevices are carefully stopped with well-tempered clay, and the building is finished."

—Michael Proctor, *Notes and Observations on America*, 183?

This well-preserved saddlebag log house was built with chimneys at each gable end and symmetrical rooms. It is part of the slave cabin quarters on Andrew Jackson's Hermitage Plantation.

common because it was hard to find replacement panes. So homeowners would stuff them with "patches of paper, and old rags, worn-out straw hats, and cast-off bonnets, pieces of thin board, and bundles of straw." The front yards of Federal or Greek Revival houses might be "studded with the stumps of trees, overgrown with rank weeds, or rutted by hogs," as James Flint said.

Inside some of these houses were few or no interior walls and no plaster on walls, Bell said. Furniture might consist of two or three beds, a large table, some "gaudily painted chairs" in the parlor, and several more crudely made chairs for everyday use. Three out of four houses in the communities he passed through weren't finished, he estimated. And not one house in 10 had a "backhouse," or privy, he added.

Built around 1835, this story-and-a-half log house is covered with clapboards and has an inset porch, along with two rooms on the first floor. The ell is a later addition, as are the turkeys.

CABINS, HUTS, AND LOG HOUSES

One of the most arresting visions of the log house in the American West is from Frances Wright, the English social reformer. "During the summer nights" families often removed the clay chinking between the logs to get better ventilation, she wrote in 1818. A traveler coming upon one of these houses at night, with candles lit or a fire going inside, had an extraordinary sight. With light spilling out of every crevice, the "log hut" glowed from within "in the darkness of the forest."

The origins of American log architecture aren't completely clear. Settlers in the West brought Scandinavian, German, and northern England traditions of log construction, and scholars dispute which had the most influence on how Americans built. Regardless of which group is most responsible, by the late 1700s, Americans of every variety were building log houses.

Many were casually dismissive about log building. The *Pictorial Geography* wrote that little skill was needed to build with logs, "for there are neither pillars for ornament, nor posts for support." The truth is, though, that log houses varied considerably in how well they were built and the skills needed to construct them.

⚜ EVERYDAY LIFE ⚜

A Fire in the Woods

Near Chillicothe, Ohio, November 22, 1818: "About a mile distant from the house where I lodged, the woods were on fire. It was supposed that the conflagration had been begun by some mischievous person, who had kindled the dry leaves, now strewed over the ground. In the evening, the glare of light extending along a ridge for a mile and a half, was astonishingly grand. Large decayed trees were converted into luminous columns of fire; when these fell the crashing noise was heard within doors. Fires in the woods usually excite alarm in their neighbourhood. People watch them by night, their rail fences and wooden habitations being in danger."
—James Flint, *Letters from America 1818–1820*

(top) Built near the banks of the Missouri River near Jefferson City, Missouri, this one-room cabin has a small upstairs loft, a later frame shed addition, and logs that are hewn flat on two sides. The original external chimney has been removed.

(bottom) This stone tavern in Switzerland County, Indiana, was built in 1811 to serve the ferry crossing on the Ohio River.

Thaddeus Mason Harris of Massachusetts discovered these differences when he crossed Pennsylvania's Allegheny Mountains in 1802: "The temporary buildings of the first settlers in the wilds are called cabins. They are built with unhewn logs." These could be thrown up fairly fast, sometimes in only a few days. To most on the Western frontier, a true log house was built of carefully squared logs dovetailed at the corners, with any crevices plastered over. "A log-house has glass windows and a chimney," while "a cabin has commonly no window at all, and only a hole at the top for the smoke to escape," Harris wrote. That made sense to Westerners, but everybody else used the terms cabin, log house, and hut interchangeably.

Anne Royall liked log houses. Those she saw on the banks of the Mississippi from the deck of her steamboat "were my delight," she wrote in 1828, reminding her of the "still independence and rural simplicity" of her Pennsylvania childhood. Onboard a Mississippi River steamboat bound for Cincinnati, she recorded her encounters with these "huts" and their families.

Close to the mouth of the Ohio River, the boat tied up for repairs near "some old shackling houses upon the brink of the river." To kill time, a passenger began to play his violin. Then "a young woman began to dance, barefooted as she was . . . and danced into the cabin, praising the music. . . . The mother, who was looking on, said, 'If they would bring the fiddle in there, she would dance too.'" The household also included several children and a couple of men, "all barefooted and bareheaded." Outside, the dilapidated house had "an old bridle, a sifter and a sheepskin" tacked to a wall and an old outdoor table "covered with a soiled cloth." They were "fine, healthy looking people and seemed to be happy and contented."

Royall greeted Western life with more equanimity and acceptance than most travelers. On an overnight stop in Illinois, she spent the night in a small cabin, "its floor four inches thick with mud" and occupied by "a loom, two beds, a dirty child and two or three pigs, a man and his wife, and his wife's sister, and as if this were not enough, two great dogs." But she enjoyed her stay and praised the farm's sizable crops and large herd of cattle. "All this was well enough," she thought. Neither husband nor wife could read, but at that time they were beginning work on a framed house.

In Connersville, Indiana, Royall reunited with a brother she hadn't seen in decades. He lived in a small frame house with a loft that had "but one room to the house below stairs, or rather below ladder." She liked this, too. "It was rural, it was wild—was what I had been used to." The

only problem it presented was that she needed a place to write. She found a ruinous log cabin nearby—the predecessor of the current house—and used it as a study during her stay.

In contrast, Frances Trollope was aghast at what she saw on the banks of the Mississippi once her northbound steamboat had passed the land of great plantations. On the Arkansas and Tennessee shores, she observed the tiny houses of the woodcutters who supplied the river steamboats with fuel. Built up on piles above high water, they were "sad dwellings," she wrote, often flooded at high water.

(top) Captain Charles Ames came to northwest Indiana from Massachusetts and built what he knew and was comfortable with: a typical New England house. The story-and-a-half central-chimney structure dates to 1842.

(right) This strikingly stark church was built in about 1840 for a Freewill Baptist congregation in Colebrook, Ohio. Going inside, a visitor would have noticed an oddity—the pulpit was at the front of the building to one side of the door.

(top) *Although this Washington County house has only a single story, its Greek Revival detail would have made it stand out among the log houses common to early Arkansas in the 1830s.*

(bottom) *A stone fireplace is located on the gable-end wall of a log house in Benton County, Missouri. The firebricks at the back are not original.*

Trollope described "the miserable wives and children of these men" as having sickly, "blueish white" complexions, the signs of chronic malaria. On one occasion, she actually spent a night in a log house but was terribly irked by bedrooms without proper ceilings that rained down wood chips, floors covered with loose planks, and log and clay chimneys that caught fire "at least a dozen times a day."

VISIONS OF OHIO

Timothy Flint, who was born in Massachusetts but spent more than a decade in Kentucky, passed through northern Ohio for the first time in 1818 and found it very familiar. In the Washington County town of Marietta, he noticed that "in the forms of the houses and the arrangements about them, you discover that this is an establishment from New England." There were one-story and two-story frame central-chimney houses that immediately reminded him of home. In addition, "moderate and equal size farms," he wrote, were dispersed over the land, "copies of the New England pattern."

The prevalence of schools, the style of churches, even the melodies of church hymns evoked his boyhood memories of New England. Ohioans had "habits of neighbourhood, to form villages and live in them" that were completely different from Kentuckians, who preferred to keep some distance between themselves and their neighbors.

Another Flint—James Flint, a visiting Englishman and no relation to Timothy—found in Ohio the hardest-working farmers and the fewest "idle men lounging in taverns" he had ever seen. He also noticed women "with dresses composed of the muslins of Britain, the silks of India, and the crapes of China"—even women living in log cabins.

Zerah Hawley of Connecticut, by contrast, hated Ohio. Ashtabula County, where he stayed for a year, was part of Connecticut's Western Reserve, land granted to the state for giving up its territorial claims in 1785. A young, unmarried physician, he had little positive to say about Ohio's northeastern corner. He saw only a "few marks of wealth, and so frequent and so great appearance of poverty and distress." For instance, the Presbyterian church in Austinburg had a steeple but no bell, no paint, and no pews; worshippers stood or sat on the floor. Families came with crockery but within a few years had broken most of it and found it hard to replace. He inquired of one acquaintance how his wife was and heard that "Oh, she's well, but barefoot, and has not had a pair of shoes for six months . . . she almost wishes herself back to the State of New-York."

There were "a few comfortable framed houses," but most settlers lived in one-room and two-room log houses. Many of the one-room houses had no fireplace, a "log being laid against the logs of the house and the fire built in front." Over the course of a few years, he said, this meant that the logs on the chimney wall were badly burnt, sometimes completely destroyed.

He also found two-room dogtrot houses. To his New England eye, they looked more like "two houses standing near each other, and covered by one roof, than one house." The dogtrot passage—so useful as a breezeway in Alabama—infuriated him in the cold Ohio climate. In winter, it made for a miserable walk between rooms. And free-running hogs trundled through the passageway every night looking for food and knocking over barrels, pots, and kettles that were stored outside.

But the absolutely worst sort of house, Hawley decided, was what the people of the vicinity called a shanty. Smaller even than the standard cabin, it was "a hovel about ten feet by eight" built with a sloping cow-shed roof. Much of the interior was taken up by a single bed where at its foot there was usually space "for a barrel or two." Shanty doors had to open outward.

As far as Hawley was concerned, no log house could be kept clean: "It is utterly impossible that neatness should exist," he wrote his brother. The clay chinking between the logs was always falling out, pieces of bark were peeling off the underside of the roof, and the family was constantly tracking in mud. "This is not an exaggerated picture," he summed up, "but a reality." In the town of Wrightsbury, he did find the best finished house in the region. It was painted white, and all the rooms were plastered and painted. Still, it did not give him much confidence that things would improve. He decided against making Ohio his home and returned to Connecticut. Ohio presented "a state of society to which I am not accustomed and in which I am unwilling to live."

The usually hypercritical Frances Trollope had a far more favorable experience with Ohio log houses when she visited a farm a few miles from Cincinnati. She found the family in a two-room log house with "a little shanty or lean-to" for a kitchen and noticed that "both rooms were comfortably furnished with good beds, drawers, Etc." When the family showed her their spinning wheels, loom, and equipment for making their own soap, candles, and shoes, Trollope thought they were a perfect example of frontier self-sufficiency. But, in fact, their comparative comfort was a result of their proximity to Cincinnati and its stores. When they really needed something, her hostess explained, they "could send a batch of butter and chickens to market."

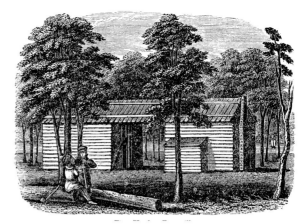

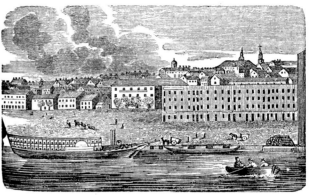

(top) Despite its impressive name, the Zanesville Hotel in central Ohio pictured around 1860, was just a log dogtrot house.

(bottom) An 1840 woodcut of Cincinnati shows a river steamboat and flatboat, as well as the thriving commerce that made it the most important city in the Western States.

CINCINNATI: THE WESTERN CAPITAL

Cincinnati was the most important city in the West. By 1840, with more than 46,000 people, it was the sixth-largest city in America, bigger than Albany, Providence, and Charleston. It "may be called the western capital of the Federal Republic," William Newnham Blane had written a few years earlier. "A more beautiful site can hardly be imagined. Steep and lofty hills touch the river at each end of the town, and encircle it behind."

Cincinnati was the West's great inland river port on the Ohio River, connected by boat and barge to New Orleans, a thousand miles downstream; to Pittsburgh, 500 miles upstream; and by road and river to a huge hinterland of farms. Coming in on a steamboat in 1819, James Flint saw the Cincinnati shore

(top) The first Presbyterian minister in Cincinnati, the Rev. James Kemper, built this log house in 1804. It is a two-story double-pen log house, with two massive chimneys, two front doors, and a second-floor side porch. Long ago moved off its original site, it is now in the Cincinnati Zoological Gardens.

(right) Joseph Ferris was one of three brothers who came to Ohio from Connecticut in 1799. Around 1820, he built this large brick central-hallway house in the countryside around Cincinnati. The porch and offset two-story addition, likely an office, came later, though probably before 1850.

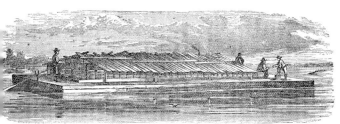

FLATBOAT FROM ST. LOUIS TO NEW ORLEANS, TIME FOUR MONTHS.

River flatboats had shallow keels to navigate low water and avoid "snags," or submerged trees and debris. Flatboatmen were often thought of as reckless and violent, but they moved thousands of tons of goods every year on the rivers of the Western States. It took a flatboat about four months to travel down the Mississippi from St. Louis to New Orleans.

"lined with keel boats, large arks for carrying produce, family boats, and rafts of timber." Once ashore, he saw the same bustle of business in the streets of the town. Scores of wagons hauled imported goods, salt, iron, and timber up from the wharves. Others brought down pork and flour to be sent to New Orleans.

Carriages and carts were noisy in the streets. The city's carpenters, blacksmiths, and coopers made "a busy din." Flint was surprised to discover that the city had few log houses. Nearly all were "brick and timber." It was an energetic urban scene that was unexpected "amongst the back woods of America." Just a year earlier, Elias Pym Fordham had noticed a few "dwellings with their proud porticos, that look too aristocratic by half for the State of Ohio."

Frances Trollope arrived in the city in 1827 and spent a year and a half there. She was also impressed with the city's "constant improvements," and remarked on how common it was to see houses being moved from place to place. The largest house that she saw in

⊛ EVERYDAY LIFE ⊛

Everyday Death

"When a person dies, a minister, if there be one at hand, is invited to preach a funeral sermon, or rather to make a funeral oration, or if no minister be near, some other gifted person undertakes the task; which is delivered to the assembled neighbours before they leave the house with the corpse. All further ceremony is commonly dispensed with, and the body is put in the ground, often not in the churchyard, or other common burying place, but in the garden, orchard, or paddock, or perhaps in the neighbouring bush, and there, not always to rest till the general resurrection, but to be raised again at a more convenient time, to be again interred in a more suitable place. Hence the gloominess of the landscape is increased, by a number of public and private cemeteries; which further sickens the mind of the already sullen, and disappointed aspirant after a visionary happiness in a strange land."

—Michael Proctor,
Notes and Observations on America, 183?

(top) This small brick row house with four rooms was probably built for a Cincinnati craftsman's family.

(bottom) Andrew Jackson owned slaves on his Tennessee plantation and was even sometimes described as an indulgent owner. This saddlebag log house is part of the quarters at the Hermitage.

motion was a two-story frame house with eight rooms, raised up on wheels and pulled by 40 oxen. "The first few yards brought down the two stacks of chimneys," she wrote, "but it afterwards went on well." These moves were particularly common when a family decided to replace a wooden house with a brick one. Then, said Trollope, it was common to see the former residence not torn down but "creeping quietly out of town" to a new location on the outskirts of the city.

However, Trollope also found much to dislike in Americans' manners and domestic arrangements. She was annoyed by their inquisitiveness, their informality, and the un-English way they cooked and furnished their houses. She used Cincinnati as a prime example of these faults, and added to her list of complaints the omnipresence of pigs (before Chicago, Cincinnati was America's pork-butchering and meat-packing capital, and the animals were everywhere—on the streets as well as in the stockyards). Her unsparing critique, *The Domestic Manners of the Americans,* was published in 1832 and was widely read on both sides of the Atlantic. No Americans were more offended than the people of Cincinnati, who took it as a betrayal of their hospitality and an affront to civic pride.

The always eccentric Anne Royall had an even less flattering view of the city. An independent-minded widow and America's first female journalist, Royall had persistence, strong views, and no tact whatsoever. Her notoriety, and the fact that she traveled without a male companion, meant that she was sometimes denied access to "respectable" taverns and hotels and therefore wound up in some tough and difficult places. During her stay in Cincinnati in 1830, she experienced the riverfront life of the boatmen and the city's poorest families. The city was "a perfect rogue's harbor," she wrote, full of "drunkenness, gambling, lewdness." It was the handsomest town in the West, she admitted, but also the wickedest.

Arriving in 1841, Charles Dickens was far less interested in the city's economic role or moral status than in how it met his novelist's gaze. Perhaps making amends for Trollope, he wrote that it was "a beautiful city, cheerful, thriving and animated." He saw "clean houses of red and white . . . well paved roads . . . pretty villas" and "well kept gardens."

Bringing Old Habits to a New Country

"The treatment of slaves is understood to be much milder in Kentucky than in the south-easterly part of the Union," James Flint wrote, adding that it was still bad enough. In the West, a region so devoted to the pursuit of individual freedom and opportunity, slavery was both self-contradictory and thriving.

Because there weren't as many slaves in Kentucky, Tennessee, Missouri, and Arkansas as there were in the Deep South, people in the Northeast tended to pay Western slavery less attention. But its marks were unmistakable. Thousands of settlers had emigrated with their slaves and reestablished the regime in the West. The river boundaries that separated Missouri and Illinois, or Ohio and Kentucky, also divided slave and free.

(above) The Hermitage was the home of Andrew Jackson, who served as the seventh President from 1828–36. His imposing house near Nashville was begun in 1818. The remarkable Greek Revival portico and wings were added in 1834–5. The house has a two-story central hall with two one-story wings.

(right) The two-story brick slave quarters of Wickland in Nelson County, Kentucky is unusually well finished for slave housing. It may have been more comfortable than most slave housing, although it's not known how many people were living there at any one time. It's unclear whether the window openings originally contained no sash, only movable shutters or were later remodeled.

20-30

(top) A view of the Mt. Lebanon Plantation in Paris, Kentucky, shows the kitchen, privy, and slave quarters to the far right and a stone-walled enclosure around a small family cemetery.

(right) The main house of the North-cut Plantation in Warren County, Tennessee, is a brick central-hallway I house. Part of a large ell is visible at the back.

Two houses in Kentucky that were documented by HABS teams speak eloquently and painfully to us. Thomas Marshall's residence in Washington, Kentucky, was a two-story brick central-hallway house that took on its current form around 1800 as the residence of a prosperous landowner and county official. But the stairs to the attic led the surveyors past parlors and bedchambers to a chilling revelation—a confinement cell and a punishment room for "refractory slaves." In its floor was bolted an iron ring.

On Maysville Pike in Bourbon County sat a house called the Grange, a handsome story-and-a-half central-hall house with a Greek Revival portico dating from around 1818. Long-standing oral tradition maintains that its first owner, Ned Stone, was a slave dealer who was killed aboard a boat carrying his human cargo to New Orleans. A stone-walled dungeon with a single window was found under the center hall, probably used for confining slaves on the property until they could be sold.

A TAVERN FOR THE WEARY

Western taverns were "but such as can be supported in a new country, where more travelers desire shelter than luxury," Samuel Goodrich warned in his *Pictorial Geography*. In reality, taverns might be well run in the larger towns, but "in small villages and remote places," people passing through had to take their chances.

Traveling in Pennsylvania west of the Alleghenies in 1802, Andre Michaux found some of the taverns to be not just unpleasant but frightening. The worst place he stayed was full of men on drinking binges, "who made the most dreadful riot." Wherever he looked, "the rooms, stairs, and yard were strewed with drunken men." This encounter gave him a poor opinion of the West and Westerners. Far too many of them were tavern-haunters with "a passion for spirituous liquors," he concluded.

Adlard Welby in 1819 heaped scorn on the "houses of entertainment" where he stayed in the new state of Indiana. They were one-room log houses with small kitchen sheds, "open to every breath of the winds without, and swarming within with fleas, bugs, and other vermin." Trying to sleep one night, he was awakened not by drunken revels but by a noisy midnight prayer meeting.

James Flint was more tolerant. An American backwoods tavern, he noted in 1819, was usually a highly visible presence in the neighborhood, just as its owner was a prominent citizen. It was often a log building, although more substantial ones could be found of frame or brick, with

Country taverns were almost always attached to a working farm and run by the farmer and his family. This early 20th-century view of the Levi Springer House—an 1817 tavern on the National Road in western Pennsylvania—shows its barns and a flourishing cornfield.

(top) This tavern in Naperville, Illinois, built in 1834, was called the "Preemption House," a term that refers to a Federal law allowing settlers to occupy Indian lands pre-emptively, that is, before the settlers acquired legal title.

(bottom) This is one of the kitchens in the kitchen wing of the Huddleston House tavern in Chillicothe, Ohio. When it operated after 1839, it may well have had a cookstove.

Built in 1839, the Huddleston House was another of the large taverns that were built to serve the heavy traffic on the National Road as the road was being built through Indiana.

"a wooden piazza in front" and a tall post for the signboard. On the sign he usually saw a portrait of George Washington, Andrew Jackson, or some other notable American, though he often couldn't tell them apart without reading the name.

Flint said that there was usually a small bell attached to the roof, which was used to summon the guests to meals. Larger towns had "taverns of different qualities," but country taverns made little distinction between guests, whether at the table or sharing beds. "It has been my lot to sleep with a diversity of personages, from the driver of the stage coach, to men of considerable name."

❀ EVERYDAY LIFE ❀

Where the Spirit Caught Fire

In August 1801 at a log meetinghouse at Cane Ridge near Paris, Kentucky, a young Presbyterian minister named Barton Stone held a camp meeting, or what today would be called a revival. Attendance estimates range from 5,000 to 30,000.

The Cane Ridge meeting was the high point of what historians call the Second Great Awakening, a resurgence of spiritual concern that swept America. A number of different preachers took to the stump at Cane Ridge. One preacher who watched from the crowd was James Finley, who years later wrote of the experience in his autobiography.

"The noise was like the roar of Niagara. The vast sea of human beings seemed to be agitated as if by a storm.

I counted seven ministers, all preaching at one time, some on stumps, others on wagons.... I stepped up on a log where I could have a better view of the surging sea of humanity. The scene that then presented itself to my mind was indescribable. At one time I saw at least five hundred swept down in a moment as if a battery of a thousand guns had been opened upon them, and then immediately followed shrieks and shouts that rent the very heavens. . . . Some of the people were singing, others praying, some crying for mercy. A peculiarly strange sensation came over me. My heart beat tumultuously, my knees trembled, my lips quivered, and I felt as though I must fall to the ground."

—The Rev. James Finley,
The Autobiography of Rev. James B. Finley

When John Krepps had this tavern built, he made sure that the date—1830—and the community—Kreppsville, named after him—were inscribed on this stone near the roof. He added two symbols: the American eagle and the farmer's plough.

He went on to address a word to the multitude of European visitors who criticized Western taverns and tavern-keepers. They needed to bear with American conditions in good humor, he admonished them, keeping in mind "the thinly-settled state of the country, the high price of labour, and the great numbers of travellers."

A few travelers were happily surprised. Fortescue Cuming was pleased to find an excellent tavern in the frontier town of Pittsburgh in 1809. McCullough's was "an inn much frequented by travelers," but it was also orderly and clean, with good food and no "noise, revelry,

❀ EVERYDAY LIFE ❀

The Road West

The National Road was one of the great thoroughfares of the westward migration. Beginning in 1811, it had been constructed in stages, starting from Cumberland, Maryland, to open the Ohio Valley for settlement. By 1820 the road had passed through southwestern Pennsylvania to Wheeling, now in West Virginia. The road's Ohio section

This gracefully arched bridge in Fulton County, Ohio, spans a stream along the National Road.

was begun in 1825 and completed in 1829; by 1834 it was completed through Indiana. Commercial villages, taverns, and stagecoach stops sprang to life along the National Road as it was built.

This traveler's map from 1832 traces the road through Pensylvania, Ohio, and eastern Indiana.

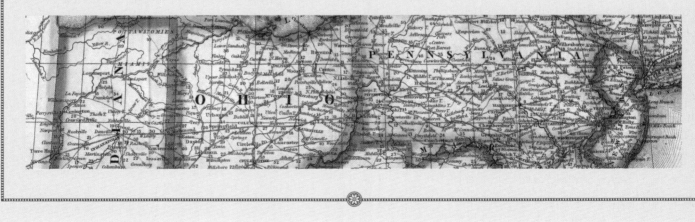

and confusion." He gave most of the credit to the "amiable and obliging" Mrs. McCullough and her three daughters, who ran a highly efficient establishment.

PLACES OF REVIVAL

Like the houses and cabins out West, the churches were also far-flung. Most were small, rough-hewn buildings maintained by widely dispersed congregations. Sometimes, church and tavern stared at each other at a rural crossroads.

Built in 1791 and well preserved today, the Cane Ridge Baptist Meetinghouse stands in Bourbon County, Kentucky. It's a simple structure of hand-hewn ash logs that measures 30 ft. by 48 ft. The building has seen more than 200 years of Sunday services and weekday prayer meetings. But in 1801 thousands of people came together for a week of worship in this remote place. The meetinghouse was at the epicenter of the great Cane Ridge Revival, an event that marked the beginning in the West of a huge wave of evangelism called the Second Great Awakening.

The most famous religious gatherings of the Western States couldn't be contained within the walls of a church. They were outdoor revivals or "camp meetings," enormous outdoor assemblies of believers for preaching, worship, repentance, and conversion.

Timothy Flint watched them closely during his stay in the Mississippi Valley. "On the appointed day," he wrote, an observer at the camp site would see "coaches, chaises, wagons, carts, people on horseback, and multitudes traveling from a distance on foot" streaming in to set up camp. Other wagons arrived with mattresses, extra tents, and provisions for a week's stay. Soon the tents began to be pitched, and "the religious city grows up in a few hours under the trees, beside the stream." Usually a group of men had arrived earlier to cut down trees and clear a large enough space.

Witnesses were never neutral about camp meetings, which turned into collective outpourings of religious emotion that often ran day and night. Believers sobbed, cried aloud, spoke in tongues, jerked spasmodically, or collapsed. Those accustomed to more restrained and decorous worship thought these folks "doleful curiosities."

Several observers also wrote about the power of the scene—the vast multitudes, flickering torches, long rows of tents, preachers standing on a high wooden platform so that they could be seen and heard. And there was the hymn singing, "the combined voices of a multitude, heard at the *(top) Located in the village of Naperville, Illinois, the First Baptist Church has a Greek Revival temple form without a steeple. By the 1930s, it had lost its surrounding landscape and was squeezed between two commercial buildings.*

(bottom) A story-and-a-half house in the western Pennsylvania community of Riceville has Greek Revival trim but also was a very traditional design with its two front doors and no entry hall.

dead of night," as Trollope described it, which even the most critical had to admit was extraordinary. James Flint could only say that "when the whole vast circumvened crowd lift up their voices, they outsing all music."

A COUNTRY ON THE THRESHOLD

Immense and full of contradictions, the Western States were a region of hope and disappointment, opportunity and privation, even of slavery and freedom.

By 1840, the Western States, from Ohio to Arkansas, had developed some vigorous cities, many thriving villages and substantial plantations, and hundreds of thousands of scattered farms. No self-governing nation had ever sought to span such a vast territory. No emigrants had ever filled up a new land so quickly or with such confidence in the future.

Before the railroad and the telegraph, the territory was vast in a way now impossible to imagine. And travelers could only hope to get a partial glimpse of the real West. Its towns, farms, houses, and people were changing too fast to be fully captured or even understood.

The way westward was never easy and often dangerous. Movers often found suffering and disappointment. In Cincinnati, Timothy Flint was reminded of this when he encountered men and women and their despairing families who had been defeated by the journey, many dying from the strain. Most, of course, survived and found some measure of success and independence. (Slaves who moved west with their owners were the tragic exception.) The most fortunate and best prepared found Ohio, Kentucky, or Illinois the country of their dreams.

Constant moving on and settling anew made the Western States a restless place. For some, moving became not just a path to a better life but an end in itself. Travelers noticed some houses only partially furnished because their inhabitants were in constant readiness to sell out, travel some miles farther, and start up all over again.

HABS No. WVA-116

The settling the West was a great and momentous migration. But from the point of view of homes and families, it was immensely difficult. And the difficulty fell harder on women than it did on men, who had greater freedom and mobility. Illinois, a local saying went, was heaven for men and horses but hell for women and cattle. The effort required to hack a farm from the forest could daunt even the strongest, and the loneliness of the woods troubled many who were used to the daily life of friends and community back home.

Through cycles of improvement and disappointment, emigrant families persisted because they had made a commitment to their family's future. The forest would soon become a farmstead. The one-room log house would become a respectable house with parlors and bedchambers. If not always for the parents, then for the children.

(top) William Renick took his stone I house of 1790 and had a brick addition constructed after 1820. The result was a gigantic two-story portico absurdly out of scale with the rest of the house.

(right) This small but elegant one-story Greek Revival house was constructed near the shores of Lake Michigan in the mid-1840s in Waukegan, Illinois.

Afterword

While writing this book, I felt that I was retracing the steps of two different groups of explorers. First in time were the visitors and writers who described the houses and landscapes of the early American republic. Then, coming to their task a hundred years later were the architects and photographers of the Historic American Building Survey. All of them became historical traveling companions.

The foreign travelers and American commentators whose observations I used in this book were a diverse and opinionated group of men and women. What they had in common was a deep interest in the American scene and a habit of careful description. Although their biases were sometimes exasperating, they were good company.

Edward Parry in 1775 and Margaret Hall in 1828 turned a disapproving but inquisitive British eye on their American surroundings. The New Englander Timothy Dwight described his own region's houses while lavishing abuse on the houses of his New York Dutch neighbors. Benjamin Rush introduced the Pennsylvania Germans to a wider American audience, because they so rarely spoke for themselves. Nathaniel Hawthorne and Herman Melville used their own houses as fictional characters. The Scotsman Peter Neilson enjoyed his southern travels, was untroubled by slavery, and provided a fascinating account of his months in Charleston. The English actress Frances Kemble married into a slave-owning family and found the domestic life of a plantation mistress unbearable. Ann Royall was unique among travelers to the Western States because she actually enjoyed staying in log cabins. Thomas Jefferson disliked all American architecture, except his own.

The hundreds of pictures in this book are a small fraction of the vast HABS collection in the Library of Congress. Choosing which ones to include from this abundance of riches was not easy. A few photographs were overexposed or blurry; some were poorly composed and without pictorial interest. But that left an enormous number of striking visual documents. We tried to choose pictures that represented the American housing landscape, that reflected what our travelers were describing, and that might not have been seen before.

One discovery was that in typically American fashion, each state's HABS office had taken a slightly different path. Boston's early houses were less well-documented than those of

Philadelphia, Charleston, and New Orleans. Alabama's photographers often asked current residents to pose outside their houses, something rarely done elsewhere. New York sometimes included staff members in the frame, catching them in the act of measuring a house. Virginia and Pennsylvania recorded many more small houses than did Massachusetts and Connecticut, while those states were far better at documenting their schools and churches.

For me, the most stunning image chosen for this book is an unnamed photographer's vision of Green Hill Plantation in Campbell County, Virginia, its buildings spread out across the landscape to create "the look of a village" that early travelers saw. But there were many others. I'm still haunted by the spectral ruins of the George Jacobs House in Danvers, Massachusetts, a reminder of family betrayal and the witchcraft trials that haunted New England into the 1800s. I was captivated by the intricate brickwork of Lower Alloways, New Jersey, seeing how the houses themselves spelled out the meanings of marriage, family, and property. A far more sobering experience was to look at Edward Stone's handsome 1818 house in Bourbon County, Kentucky, and realize that as fine as it appears, it had been built with a slave dungeon in the basement. A striking photograph captures children playing in front of a traditionally built log schoolhouse in Sevier County, Tennessee. And why, I still wonder, did the owners of the Hazelwood estate in Prince George's County, Maryland, decide to combine a privy and a smokehouse in a single building?

The HABS collection is a national treasure, whose true glory is that it is open for all of us to explore on the Library of Congress's American Memory website.

Why should we care about old houses or about the past in general? Americans have not always been sure. In the years of the new nation, Americans were proud to be a "go-ahead" people plunging into the future; most of them thought little about the past in their rush to build something new. Fortunately, they left a historical record behind anyway.

Today, an increasing number of Americans want to find meaning, inspiration, and challenge in their history. The history of old houses and vanished landscapes is one part of that history. The past anchors us.

RESOURCES

For a general view of life in the early United States, you might turn to Jack Larkin, *The Reshaping of Everyday Life 1790-1840* (New York: HarperCollins, 1989). For a readable and authoritative introduction to architectural history, Dell Upton, *Architecture in the United States* (New York: Oxford, 1998). Henry Glassie's books about ordinary people's houses are full of interesting ideas: *Vernacular Architecture* (Bloomington: Indiana University, 2000) and *Pattern in the Material Folk Culture of the Eastern United States* (Philadelphia: University of Pennsylvania Press, 1968 & still in print). For looking at houses, there are many guidebooks. Two useful ones are Virginia Lee Macalester and others, *A Field Guide to American Houses* (New York: Knopf, 1984) and John G. Blumenson, *Identifying American Architecture: A Pictorial Guide to Styles and Terms: 1600-1945* (New York: Norton, 1981).

Exploring the resources of the Historic American Buildings Survey is easy, thanks to the American Memory website of the Library of Congress. The URL for the HABS database is http://memory.loc.gov/ammem/collections/habs_haer/.

Once there, you can browse by PLACE: state, county, and community. For example, if you start with Alabama, you will find entries starting with Ataraugus County and ending with Wilcox County. Each entry will contain links to photographs and/or drawings (often both) and (usually) pages of description and historical information.

You can also browse by SUBJECT. You will find a huge alphabetical list, from "abandoned buildings" to "zoos." This is not a perfect search process, because it depends on what words were literally in the HABS records. So "abandoned buildings" will take you to some entries, and "ruins" will take you to others.

Or you can go to the SEARCH window and find things more directly. You can search for a building by its owner's name; to avoid duplication you will want to add information about state, county and community. You could enter "log Missouri" to find log structures in Missouri or "church Portage Ohio" to find churches in Portage County, Ohio.

The American Memory website will also let you explore the experiences of many of men and women who traveled through early America. Go to American Memory and click on "American Notes: Travels in America 1750-1820" and you will have access to over a hundred travelers' accounts. (Its URL is http://memory.loc.gov/ammem/lhtnhtml/lhtnhome.html.)

Finally, you will be able to find a wealth of information about houses, history and preservation available from the National Trust for Historic Preservation, at http://www.nationaltrust.org.